Virtual Worlds for Language Learning

TELECOLLABORATION IN EDUCATION

Vol. 2

Edited by
Melinda Dooly & Robert O'Dowd

PETER LANG
Bern · Berlin · Bruxelles · Frankfurt am Main · New York · Oxford · Wien

Randall Sadler

Virtual Worlds for Language Learning

From Theory to Practice

PETER LANG
Bern · Berlin · Bruxelles · Frankfurt am Main · New York · Oxford · Wien

Bibliographic information published by die Deutsche Nationalbibliothek
Die Deutsche Nationalbibliothek lists this publication in the Deutsche Nationalbibliografie; detailed bibliographic data is available on the Internet at ‹http://dnb.d-nb.de›.

British Library Cataloguing-in-Publication Data: A catalogue record for this book is available from The British Library, Great Britain

Library of Congress Cataloging-in-Publication Data

Sadler, Randall,
Virtual worlds for language learning : from theory to practice / Randall Sadler.
p. cm. – (Telecollaboration in education ; v. 2)
Includes bibliographical references.
ISBN 978-3-03-430573-0
1. Languages, Modern–Computer-assisted instruction. 2. Shared virtual environments.
3. Virtual reality in education. I. Title.
PB35.S23 2012
418.007–dc23
2012011750

ISBN (pb) 978-3-0343-0573-0 ISBN (eBook) 978-3-0351-0406-6

Hochfeldstrasse 32, CH-3012 Bern, Switzerland
info@peterlang.com, www.peterlang.com

Contents

Series Editors' Preface

This series is dedicated to promoting a wider understanding of the activity of telecollaboration in educational settings. Telecollaboration refers to the pedagogical processes and outcomes of engaging learners in different geographical locations in virtual contact together, mediated through the application of online communication tools such as e-mail, synchronous chat and threaded discussion as well as the tools of Web 2.0 such as wikis, blogs, social networking and 3D virtual worlds. The application of such activity may include different subject areas (e.g. Foreign Language Education, History, Science) as well as different educational contexts, including but not limited to primary, secondary, university and adult education.

This second volume in our series looks at a key theme in the area of foreign language education in recent years: the potential of Virtual Worlds (VWs) for foreign language-based interaction and exchange. It is almost axiomatic to say that major forces of change are defying us to accommodate to new ideas of learning that leverage technologies and human capital in new ways. Teachers are facing challenges to adapt to new understandings of not only how learning takes place, but also new concepts of how and where learning occurs—in the 'real' world or in simulated worlds where learners are physically distributed across the globe but gathered together through 3D representations of selves.

Virtual worlds are already being touted as relevant foreign language learning environments because they are engaging and motivating for learners and, at the same time, a cost-effective means of bringing authentic elements into the learning process (albeit 'simulated authentic' but still closer to the 'real thing' than many language classrooms). Educators also put forth the benefits of virtual worlds for collaborative learning. Picking up on this theme, this book explores the potential for virtual worlds in telecollaborative language learning.

As Bruns (2008) points out, online networked culture has the potential to radically alter the ways in which people interact with the media—and one might add, with educational institutions. This interaction is captured in Brun's term of 'produsage': people working together to solve problems from ground up; traditional hierarchies are overturned for ad hoc meritocracies; small tasks are contributed by individuals to complete larger-scale activities and, eventually, the final outcome is shared for mutual benefits. These key concepts of interaction are evoked and exemplified by the author so that the reader can envision different possibilities for 'produsage' practices in teaching languages in virtual worlds that fit into the paradigm of socioconstructivist learning.

This book provides an indispensable introduction to the participatory culture of virtual worlds in language learning for teachers who are interested in exploring this potentially rich environment. It sets out the various affordances of virtual worlds (including gaming) for language learning and even those practitioners who are already engaged in VWs will find the book's content informative in its wide scope of described environments. There is ample discussion on how to conceptualise telecollaborative language learning, task design and assessment in virtual environments, sprinkled with informed anecdotes and case studies that help exemplify topics that would otherwise be quite abstract. This volume contributes insightful reflections on innovative aspects of online language pedagogy—based on telecollaboration in virtual worlds—that will be of interest now and in the future, as these 'new' worlds become more firmly entrenched in our everyday lives.

Melinda Dooly, Universitat Autònoma de Barcelona, Spain
Robert O'Dowd, Universidad de León, Spain

12 November 2011

References:

Bruns, A. (2008). *Blogs, wikipedia, second life, and beyond: From production to produsage*. Bern: Peter Lang.

Acknowledgements

I would like to acknowledge the many individuals I have worked with both in Virtual Worlds like Second Life and also in the Real World who helped to make this book happen. When I was a noob in Second Life, wandering about virtually dazed and confused, there were many gracious avatars—both educators and other explorers—who took me under their wings and helped me to understand the potential of the many virtual spaces we now have available. While it is simply not possible to put together a complete list of those individuals (who number in the many hundreds), there are a few I would like to thank in particular.

First, Melinda Dooly (Melinda Aristocrat in Second Life) has been generous enough to bring groups of students into SL from the Universitat Autonòma de Barcelona (UAB) to work with my students at the University of Illinois at Urbana-Champaign. This interaction formed a basis for the creation of this book, and made me consider a number of pedagogical aspects of teaching in VWs that would never have occurred to me otherwise. She is an excellent education and research partner.

I'd also like to acknowledge the work of several individuals on the EduNation islands in Second Life, first Heike Philp (Gwen Gwasi in SL) and Carol Rainbow (Carolrb.roux in SL). Heike is the co-owner (with me) of the EduNation islands in SL—and a constant source of pedagogical inspiration. Carol has worked tirelessly to help make those islands the wonderful educational environment that they are today. Teaching opportunities in SL would be poorer without both of them! I'd also like to thank Graham Davies (Groovy Winkler), the head of the EUROCALL SIG for Virtual Worlds and the lead decorator for the joint EUROCALL/CALICO Headquarters in SL. His sense of humor and excellent knowledge always make the islands a great place to be.

Special thanks as well to my wife, Misumi, who puts up with my many hours spent online in SL. Her patience and understanding made this book possible.

Chapter 1: Introduction

> The matrix has its roots in primitive arcade games [...] Cyberspace. A consensual hallucination experienced daily by billions of legitimate operators, in every nation, by children being taught mathematical concepts [...]. A graphic representation of data abstracted from banks of every computer in the human system. Unthinkable complexity. Lines of light ranged in the nonspace of the mind, clusters and constellations of data. Like city lights, receding into the distance [...]. (Gibson, *Neuromancer*, 1984)

What are Virtual Worlds?

When William Gibson coined the term cyberspace in his novel *Neuromancer* (1984), the Internet as we now know it did not yet exist. While some of the concepts discussed in that novel are still in the realm of fantasy, others, such as the "consensual hallucination" of Virtual Worlds, are now among the most popular activities available online.

Some might argue that a new technology hits the mainstream when Hollywood decides to make a movie about it. In the case of Virtual Worlds (VWs) the past few years have seen several blockbusters. In 2010, the movie *Avatar* became the best-selling movie of all time, telling the story of a man who used another body—his avatar—to exist in a new world. In 2009, *Surrogates*, starring Bruce Willis, told the story of a future world where the humans stayed home, and their idealized robot bodies (their surrogates, or avatars) went out into the world. Earlier, *The Matrix* (1999) told the story in reverse, with the humans existing as avatars in a Virtual World and not knowing it, only to discover the truth when freed from that virtual reality. For many of us, our first introduction to a VW may have been in *Star*

Trek: The Next Generation (1987), where the holodeck could take crew members to almost any world, whether "real" or imaginary. Of course, long before most of these, Jeff Bridges was pulled against his will into another Virtual World in *Tron* (1982), where he battled with programs who often resembled their real world creators. This world was revisited in 2010 (*Tron: Legacy*).

Long before VWs appeared on the screen in theaters or televisions, they were formed via the written word in novels and short stories. In 1935 Stanley Grauman Weinbaum wrote *Pygmalion's Spectacles* in which one of his characters—Professor Albert Ludwig—created a new type of movie that foresees the evolution of Virtual Worlds and Virtual Reality as they are experienced today. He describes this technology to Dan, the protagonist of the story:

> 'Listen! I'm Albert Ludwig—Professor Ludwig.' As Dan was silent, he continued, 'It means nothing to you, eh? But listen—a movie that gives one sight and sound. Suppose now that I add taste, smell, even touch, if your interest is taken by the story. Suppose I make it so that you are in the story, you speak to the shadows, and the shadows reply, and instead of being on a screen, the story is all about you, and you are in it. Would that be to make real a dream?'

This exploration of what we now think of as VWs continued in novels and stories like Victor Vinge's *True Names* (1981) William Gibson's *Neuromancer* (1984), and Neal Stephenson's *Snow Crash* (1992). Indeed, *Neuromancer* included a description of "the matrix" and "Zion" almost fifteen years before they appeared again in modified form in the movie starring Keanu Reeves. Interestingly, while all of these works are located solidly in the "science fiction" area of many local public libraries, one of the newest novels that examines life (and murder) in a VW—*Virtually Dead* (2010) by Peter May—was found in the "fiction" area of my local library instead. This book, which takes place within the existing virtual world of Second Life™, contains elements that would have most certainly been science fiction at the time of these earlier works; elements that have become reality today.

Virtual Worlds as we understand them today are three-dimensional (3-D) computer-based environments that can be used for a wide variety of purposes. One of the most familiar is WoW (World of Warcraft™), which is traditionally not used for education—unless your education is focused on swords, maiming, and killing elves and ogres (although this type of environment, as discussed in the next chapter, may certainly be used for educational purposes as well). However, other Virtual Worlds, such as Second Life, Habbo, Active Worlds, Club Penguin, etc. have a different philosophy. These worlds tend to exist primarily as social environments, with (at least in some) most of the content created by the very people who "live" there. This means that these worlds can have rich social environments with activities ranging from those similar to WoW, to VW-based language schools. At their most basic, as discussed by Rheingold (1991), Virtual Reality (VR) Systems have two fundamental requirements:

> The idea of immersion—using stereoscopy, gaze-tracking, and other technologies to create the illusion of being inside a computer-generated scene—is one of the two foundations of VR technology. The idea of navigation—creating a computer model of a molecule or a city and enabling the user to move around, as if inside it—is the other fundamental element. Nothing about either of these key elements requires that they be implemented in one specific kind of technology (pp. 112–113).

As opposed to full VR, Virtual Worlds focus more strongly on the second component of Rheingold's definition. All modern VWs consist of 3-D environments in which users interact with the environment and each other. Rather than relying on the more advanced technologies such as gaze-tracking, VRs typically utilize a keyboard/mouse interface though which users move their online persona or avatar.[1]

1 For easy access to any URLs mentioned in this book and for additional resources related to Virtual Worlds and Language Learning, visit the accompanying website for this book at: <http://www.eslweb.org/virtualworlds>.

Who is this Book Written for?

The book is intended for multiple audiences, including the simply curious, teachers who wish to use a VW for their own teaching, language learners, language teachers who are interested in integrating Virtual Worlds into their telecollaboration projects, professors teaching courses related to Virtual Worlds and/or CMC, for those doing research in VWs, and (as implied in the picture) anyone reading this book. However, it begins with several important assumptions:

Figure 1.1: Avatar in SL

Some of the readers of this book will have virtually no experience with Virtual Worlds. If the reader falls into this category they are most welcome! This book will make no assumptions that the readers have explored virtual worlds or indeed that they have extensive knowledge about the use of Computer-Mediated Communication (CMC) in general.

Other readers of this book will already have extensive experience in VWs. This group will also benefit from this text since it will provide information on worlds they have not yet explored and insight into educational theories and pedagogical practices they may not be familiar with.

Finally, this book assumes a willingness on the part of the readers to actively explore in some of the VWs mentioned in the text. While the chapters outlined in the following section are an excellent starting point in understanding and using VWs for language learning or teaching, it is crucial that readers get their feet wet (or at least their virtual feet, virtually wet) as part of the process.

For those interested in using a VW in their own teaching, this book provides a firm foundation in several ways. First, it will familiarize you with the basic concepts and history of VWs. Second, it establishes a connection between VWs and language learning theory. Third, the book will provide opportunities for exploring the nexus between VWs and telecollaboration. Finally, this text connects theory to pedagogical practice. Following the information provided in this book should enable teachers to create their own educational telecollaborative environments in a VW such as Second Life. This book is also appropriate for use in either graduate or undergraduate courses designed for future language educators that focus on the use of technology in the language classroom. Indeed, the genesis for this book was my own need for a text that provided an in-depth examination of VWs in a way that I could not find in the existing literature on the topic.

This text, and the supplemental readings and websites mentioned within, will provide students with a detailed understanding of VWs and language learning theory. In addition, it will be of interest to scholars who wish to do research in the area of Virtual Worlds and Language Learning (VWLL) and Virtual Worlds and Telecollaboration (see the following chapter for a detailed discussion on telecollaboration. Finally, for those who are simply curious about Virtual

Worlds and Gaming, this text will either serve as an introduction to the topic or a richer understanding of the nuances of VWs.

How is this Book Organized?

This book is organized into six chapters, and it includes general information on VWs, the theory behind teaching in VWs, and the pedagogical applications of VWs. The first section of the book (chapters 1–3) provides an overview of Virtual Worlds and explores the theory behind using them for language learning and for their use in telecollaboration aimed at fostering language teaching and learning. In addition to the main content, each of the chapters discussed below also includes suggested additional readings and resources. Chapter 2 provides an overview and history of Virtual Worlds, including an examination of some of the current popular VWs and MMOGs, ranging from Second Life to World of Warcraft. In addition, this chapter traces the history of VWs, from MUDs to the present day. Chapter 3 explores the connections between existing educational theories and VWs, ranging from Dewey's Experiential Model (1916) to Long's Interaction Hypothesis (1981). Although these theories were not created with VWs in mind (Dewey's model long predates the computer!), this chapter will explore how such theoretical foundations can lead to strong pedagogical applications.

The second section of the book (chapters 4–6) investigates the pedagogical applications of VWs. Chapter 4 provides an in-depth overview of one of the Virtual Worlds heavily used for education—Second Life—and reports on the results of a survey conducted in that Virtual World on how languages are being used and learned in that environment. Among the questions answered are: What languages and nationalities are represented among SL users? How many SL users are participating in that VW in order to learn and/or improve their second language skills? What languages are actually being used there? How are users learning languages in SL?

Chapter 5 examines a number of potential language learning environments in SL. This includes an overview of both traditional and non-traditional educational environments, and also a number of practical pedagogical applications of VWs based on the theories discussed in Chapter 3, focusing on collaborative activities. These include activities on all 4 skills, focusing on telecollaboration, simulations, and Task-Based Language Teaching (TBLT). Chapter 6 concludes the book with a discussion areas in need of additional in-depth research, some predictions regarding the future of VWs and a list of resources.

Chapter 2: Overview and History

> Everything is backwards now, like out there is the true world and in here is the dream (Jake Sully, *Avatar*, 2010).
>
> In the virtual world you have the divine power to create life, your life, and mould it into pretty much anything you please (Winder, 2008, p. ix).

Introduction

Modern Virtual Worlds do not exist in a vacuum (except those that are set in outer space). The VWs that we may experience today are evolutions of those that came before, going back to more primitive 3D graphics, then 2D images, and finally to text-only environments. While almost none of these environments were initially specifically designed for use in language education, it is important to note that all of those discussed in this chapter have indeed been used for that purpose. After introducing some of the key terms and concepts related to Virtual Worlds, this chapter will give a brief history of the evolution of VWs and then provide an overview of some of the most popular VWs that are available today.

Key Terms and Concepts

As is often the case when dealing with matters of technology and education, there are a large number of terms—many of them seemingly random collections of letters in the form of acronyms—that are currently used in this area. In this book the term you will most often see used when referring to the 3D environments discussed here is Virtual World, but because of the numerous expressions in use this chapter will begin with definitions of a number of them.

Computer-Assisted Language Learning (CALL)

CALL is the umbrella term that describes any use of computers in the process of language learning. In earlier days, this often took the form of computer-based exercises following an Audiolingual/ Behaviorist model. The student might log into a computer program dealing with article usage (I remember spending hours—and hours—on such exercises on an Apple II™ computer) and receive a sentence like this:

_____ libro es azul.

In this case—an exercise dealing with Spanish articles—the correct response would be for the student to type el into the blank. With a correct response, the student would receive immediate feedback (positive reinforcement) along the lines of muy bien, with an incorrect response resulting in something like incorrecto appearing on the screen. CALL may also refer to the use of more advanced programs like the popular Rosetta Stone™ series, which includes the use of text, audio, and video, but still makes use of student-to-computer interaction. As a general term, CALL may also include some portions of CMC (see below). While not the focus of this text, there have been a number of excellent works examining the role of CALL, such as those by Chapelle (2001), Levy (1997), Egbert (1999), Egbert (2005), Egbert & Petrie (2005), Fotos & Browne (2004), and Levy & Stockwell (2006). All of these texts provide overviews of this important area.

Computer-Aided Instruction (CAI)

CAI is the use of computers to enhance any form of instruction. While this might include language learning, it could include instruction ranging from astronomy to zoology. A great deal of early work in this area was completed in the PLATO project (see below for more information), and was greatly influenced by the Behaviorist Traditions of learning, with the computer providing immediate feedback for learners as discussed above. The use of CAI continues today, ranging from childhood learning programs to teach reading on devices like the iPad™ to computer-based tutorials for student studying physics in college.

Computer-Mediated Communication (CMC)

In education-related discussions, CMC is most often seen as a subset of CALL, but the focus of CMC is interaction between people who are making use of computers as the facilitator for that interaction. Crook (1994) refers to this as making use of the computer as a tool to aid in communication between human participants rather than a tutor as would be the case with CALL. CMC could include any use of computers in the communication process ranging from email, to message boards, to blogs, to Virtual Worlds. Two books that examine this area are those by Barnes (2003) and Thurlow, Lengel, & Tomic (2004).

Computer-Mediated Communication for Language Learning (CMCLL)

This refers specifically to the use of CMC for the learning of language, rather than the wider potential use of CMC for business, talking with friends and family, etc. This continues to be a rich area for research, with a number of studies focused on the effect of text-based exchanges on language learning including research focused on email (e.g. Absalon & Marden, 2004; Biesenbach-Lucas & Weasenforth, 2001; Fedderholdt, 2001; O'Dowd, 2003; Shang, 2003), and message boards (e.g., Benton, 1996; Kamhi-Stein, 2000; Ware, 2004). There is also an existing body of research into synchronous forms of CMC, beginning with the use of MUDs (discussed later in this chapter) and MOOs (Kötter, 2001b; Peterson, 2001; Weininger & Shield, 2003), and on the use of other forms of text chat (e.g., Bearden, 2003; Freiermuth, 2002; Perez, 2003; Smith, 2001; Tudini, 2003; Williams, 2003). There are also a growing number of studies in this area on the effect of forms of CMC involving audio and/or video (Cziko & Park, 2003; Hampel & Hauck, 2004; Kötter, 2001a; Kötter, Shield, & Stevens, 1999; Lamy, 2004, Sadler & Eröz-Tuğa, 2009). Since some of these forms of communication (i.e., synchronous text chat, audio chat) are also used in VW interaction, the implications from these works are likely to have an impact on future research in VWs as well.

Network-Based Language Teaching (NBLT)

Often used interchangeably (and somewhat erroneously) with CMC. This term specifically refers to the use of computer networks—most often via the Internet—to enhance language learning or teaching.

Telecollaboration

O'Dowd (2006) refers to telecollaboration as the use of NBLT "to connect language learners in different countries for the development of collaborative project work and intercultural exchange" (p. 9). Unlike in the computer as tutor model discussed above, where the activities normally have a more discrete-point focus (usually on grammar), telecollaboration may focus more widely on the cultures of the groups involved in the communication and/or on discrete grammatical elements as part of that communicative process. Telecollaboration has also been defined according to other finalities it may have, apart from intercultural competence. According to Thorne (2006), telecollaboration traditionally involves language learners in geographically distant locations engaging in bilingual, bicultural exchanges. However, authors such as Dooly (2008) have argued that teachers in general, and not just those connected to language learning, have embraced the educational opportunities provided by CMC and call for a wider definition, beginning with an etymological look at the word itself: tele (distance) collaboration. For the purposes of this book, telecollaboration shall be defined as language learners (or teachers) from different geographical locations (whether those locations be in the same country or international) engaging in collaboration with their distant partners for the purpose of either culture or language exchange. While these collaborative activities could be dyadic in nature, they more often involve—again for this text—groups on both ends of the exchange.

The relationships between CAI, CALL, CMCLT, NBLT, and Telecollaboration are shown in Figure 2.1. As illustrated, there is considerable overlap between these fields, with telecollaboration situated within CMCLT.

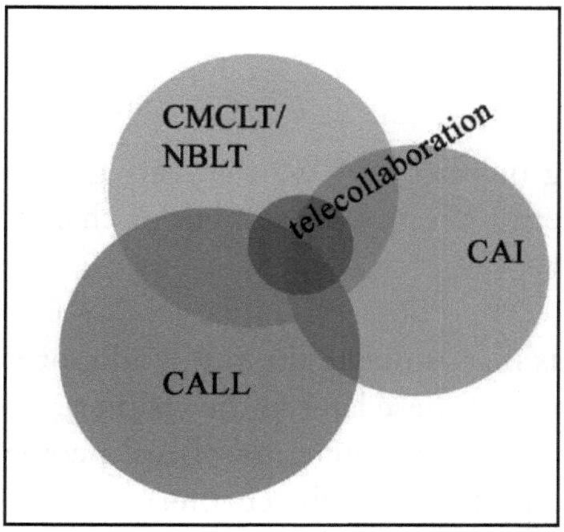

Figure 2.1: Computers, Communication, and Interaction

However, as telecollaboration is an aid in instruction, and involves the use of computers, it has potential for both CAI and CALL in general. Not all CMC falls under CALL because not all communication that is mediated via computers involves language learning. Indeed, the majority of communication that takes place via computer networks relates to business, social life, etc. and does not involve the learning of another language.

Telecollaboration for Language Learning (TlcLL)

As suggested by Figure 2.1, not all telecollaboration is directly related to language learning. For example, telecollaboration could be utilized between students enrolled in schools in the U.K. and the U.S. to discuss the history of the Second World War, with all the communication taking place in English. Since it is now apparent that many content areas are rapidly incorporating distanced-learners in collaborative learning projects, some authors have opted to instead use the more specific term of Telecollaborative Language Learning (Dooly, 2011; Lamy & Goodfellow, 2010).

Virtual World (VW)

While there are an ever-increasing number of VWs that vary greatly in terms of their content, all modern VWs share a number of characteristics. These include:

- On-line 3D environment. This may simulate the real world, or it may be wildly creative (examples of these later in the chapter).
- Avatars. Avatars are the in-world representations of real people who control them (see more on this later in the chapter).
- Real-time Interactivity. VWs include the possibility of interacting with other avatars in the environment in real time (synchronous communication), and usually with a range of objects in that VW.

- 24-hour Accessibility. As opposed to interacting with a friend via a program like Skype™, where the potential for interaction only exists as long as the program is open and both parties are connected, a VW should be open and accessible 24-hours a day.[2]
- Persistence. When a user logs out of a VW, their avatar, and the actions taken by that avatar, are not deleted.
- Social Space. Although VWs may vary in look and theme, all VWs are primarily social spaces that exist for the purpose of humans interacting via their avatars.
- Numbers. In most VWs there are many players (sometimes in the hundreds of thousands) online in the world at the same time. Given the social nature of these spaces, underpopulated VWs tend to fade away quickly as users lose interest.
- In many—though not all— VWs, users can also control their own appearance (e.g. height, facial features, eye color), gender, clothing, and even their species. In addition, many VWs allow users some control over their environment. In Second Life, for example, users have the ability to build their own home, complete with furnishing, landscaping, etc.

While the interface of VWs may sometimes seem very game-like, VWs are often used for non-gaming purposes, ranging from education, to business meetings, to commerce. A number of VWs have their own virtual currency, and some players earn their real life livelihoods solely via their work in the virtual world environment.

Multiuser Virtual Environment (MuVE)

Often used interchangeably with Virtual World.

2 In the "real world" of virtual worlds, it is more likely the case that VWs are *usually* available 24-hours a day since they are sometimes down for scheduled (or unscheduled) maintenance.

Massively Multiplayer Online Role play Game (MMORPG)

MMORPGs such as World of Warcraft have become the de facto home to a lost generation of teens. 'It's only a game' is not a phrase you are likely to hear coming from their lips; it goes way beyond play as most of us think of it. This is no fire-and-forget blast on the PlayStation, no hour wasted at the Monopoly board. To the MMORPG player this is as real as it gets (Winder, 2008: 15).

MMORPGs share all the key characteristics of VWs, as described above, but add a new required element: Role Play. While many VWs may include an element of role play (there are regions in Second Life with medieval, 1920s Chicago, or Star Trek™ themes), this is a crucial and required element of games like World of Warcraft (WoW).

Figure 2.2: World of Warcraft

Many of the most popular MMORPGs, such as WoW (See Figure 2.2), have fantasy themes, with the players (via their avatars) taking on the role of the characters they select.

Massively Multiplayer Online Game (MMOG)

Sometimes used interchangeably with MMORPG, MMOG is the general term used to refer to any game that is played online and is massively multiplayer. While many of the most popular MMOGs are also MMORPGs, this term could also include MMOGs that are focused on sports, World War II, or any theme. It could certainly be argued that these latter games also involve role play, so the two terms are sometimes used interchangeably.

Collaborative Virtual Environment (CVE)

CVEs include any virtual environments, either text-based or graphical, where collaboration is the goal. Although this has the potential to include any Virtual World (e.g., Second Life, Habbo), this category of environment would also cover message boards, wikis, or a number of MMORPGs such as WoW—since groups of avatars collaborate in WoW to eliminate other groups of avatars. Inevitably, it is this feature of collaboration that makes VWs optimal for telecollaboration in language learning. It is important to note here that it is not necessarily the environment itself that makes a VW or CVE a useful tool for educators. Instead, it is the way in which VWs can be conceived by the teachers as a tool for promoting deep, communicative language interaction that is the key factor. VWs (and associated environments) are tools—just like email or computer projectors. How teachers make use of those tools will determine whether or not successful learning will take place for their students.

Real World (RW) or Real Life (RL)

RL and RW are the terms commonly used in VWs when referring to life outside of the VW. (e.g., "I'd love to talk more, but I have to head off to RL"). Real, as discussed by Aldrich, is also:

> Being from the physical world of atoms, as opposed to the virtual world of bits. For example, real person, real world, or real money. Often the opposite of virtual. The real world can also be described condescendingly. Traditional mail is "snail mail," traditional magazines may be "dead tree publications," and the real world itself may be called the "meat" world. (Aldrich, 2009: 3)

Many users of Virtual Worlds share Aldrich's attitude that VWs are often belittled due to their game-like qualities.

Avatars

When Jake Sully, in the movie Avatar, reclines in the medical bay to interface with his avatar, his mind controls the physical construct of his N'avi/human hybrid. In The Matrix, Neo follows a similar procedure, but uses a large (and painful looking) connection jack inserted directly into his brain in order to enter the virtual environment. In a modern Virtual World (rather than the Hollywood variety) a human uses his or her mind, via a keyboard and mouse interface or some other controller, to manipulate a digital avatar in a digital world seen on a computer display. Thankfully, we have no need for direct inputs to the brain. The avatar is a key component in any Virtual World interaction.

Figure 2.3: Second Life Avatars

In a MUD or MOO (see below) the avatar is text-based, with users normally including a textual description of who they are in that virtual environment so that others may see them via that textual depiction. While that description might closely fit their real life self, it could also be radically different. In a modern VW, an avatar is a virtual 3D representation of the person controlling it. As seen in Figure 2.3, avatars (these from Second Life) have rapidly evolved.

Ruth—the avatar on the left—was one of the earliest versions of the female avatar in Second Life when it launched in 2003. The avatar on the right is Randall Renoir, my own Second Life avatar. The Ruth version of the avatar does still appear in Second Life, especially after a teleporter malfunction. This Ruth in fact, is my own avatar after just such a malfunction. Fortunately, the version you see on the right was quickly (and happily) restored. Earlier version of avatars (see Figure 2.8 below) included 2D or—as described earlier—text-based versions. Modern avatars such as those shown in Figure 2.3 are 3D creations that interact in a 3D world.

Newbie or Noob

A newbie is someone who is "new" to the VW. As seen with the Ruth avatar in Figure 2.3, noobs usually look like the default avatar that is given to new users, with the "standard" clothing, hair, shape, walk, etc. To be called a noob is not a good thing. Happily for those who have recently joined Second Life, the default avatars now supplied to new users do not look as noob as they used to.

A Brief History of the Field

To trace the history of Virtual Worlds is to trace the history of computer networks, as well as advances in computer design, graphics cards, and more. While today's 3D, graphics-intensive, avatar-based social spaces have exploded in popularity, their roots may be traced back to the earliest days of computer networks, when 3D—or even graphics—did not yet exist for computers.

Earliest Days—PLATO

Long before MUDs, MOOs, VWs, CMC, or CALL (more on these below), there was PLATO (Programmed Logic for Automated Teaching Operations).

Figure 2.4: PLATO

PLATO (see Figure 2.4) was created at the University of Illinois at Urbana-Champaign beginning in the early 1960s and was the first large-scale foray into the use of computer-assisted instruction, with over 15,000 hours of computer-based instructional materials created over the years. These included education programs that ranged from physics, to music, to second language learning, all following a Behaviorist/Audiolingual model to make use of the computers as tutors for learning.

However, PLATO went far beyond Audiolingual exercises, as it was also "a time-sharing network offering email, newsgroups, real-time chat, multiplayer games, distance learning, audio, high-resolution graphics, and touch-screen interfaces, a quarter-century before the birth of the Web" (Silberman, 1997). Readers of this book who were amazed at their first experience with the touch screen of the iPhone™ may be surprised to learn that the PLATO IV computer (seen in Figure 2.4) had a touch screen in 1972, 35 years before the introduction of the iPhone™.

PLATO's first 2-player game, Spacewar, came out in the late 1960s, long before games like Asteroids (1979) or Pac Man (1980) arrived in the newly created video arcades of the 1980s.

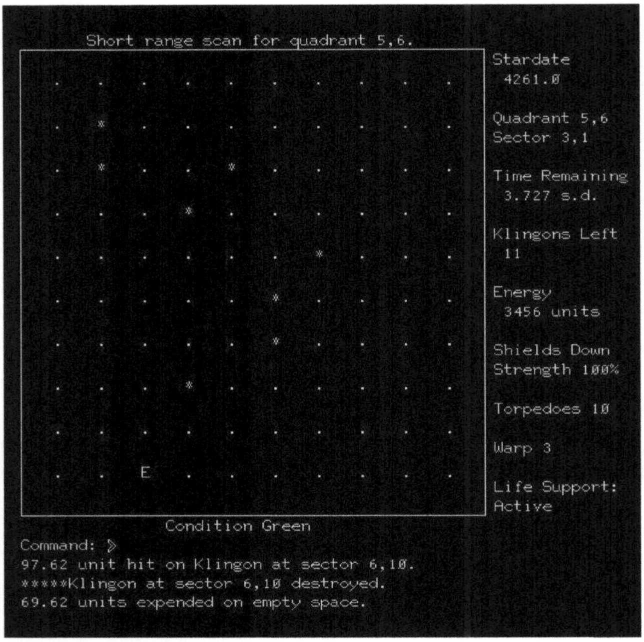

Figure 2.5: PLATO Star Trek

Spacewar was soon followed in the 1970s by multiplayer games like the Dungeons and Dragons game Avatar, and Empire, which was based on the Star Trek TV show (see Figure 2.5 for a later PLATO version of Spacewar). Ironically, Star Trek Online (a modern MMORPG) took almost 40 more years to open in 2010. In essence, all the advances that will be discussed throughout this book began with PLATO.

MUDs & MOOs

> A MUD is a multiplayer computer game that typically combines text instant message chat rooms and role-playing games. Typically, players read descriptions of their environment, objects, events, and characters in a virtual world. Users interact with other players and their surrounding by typing text commands. Many MUDs involve a fantasy world populated by mythical beings. In

> order to complete quests or adventures, users must complete tasks, while exploring the virtual world. (Childress & Braswell, 2006: 188)

Anyone who grew up in the 1970s—or at least those of us willing to admit being young nerds in the 70s—is likely to be familiar with the gaming sensation of the time called Dungeons & Dragons (D&D). During that era (and to a smaller extent even today), many teens spent far too many hours huddled in their parents' basements around a table, trading turns with many-sided dice. The fate of their character (whether it was a human, elf, wizard, or one of many other possibilities) during the game (campaign) depended on the roll of the dice, the skill of the player, and the mood of the all-powerful Dungeon-Master in charge of that day's game.

With the rise of computer networks in the 1970s, it soon became apparent to programmers that some of this D&D gaming might make use of computers and networks to take these campaigns into a new realm of action. Colossal Cave Adventure, created by Will Crowther in 1975, introduced users to a text-based environment based on a real cave system with which Crowther was very familiar. This game allowed users to interact with the computer game in a way that had not been possible before, but Adventure did not allow for interaction between multiple players with the game. This was soon followed by Zork (1977) which gained many loyal users (including yours truly).

In 1978 Roy Trubshaw created a new game called MUD, which stood for Multi-User Dungeon. This is widely credited as being the world's first Virtual World environment (though some PLATO users would disagree). Now called MUD1, a version of this VW still exists on the British-Legends website <http://www.british-legends.com> where it may still be played today. As seen in Figure 2.6, actions taken by the player in this environment result in a variety of responses by the program. In the example given in Figure 2.6 the player (the author of this book) has just foolishly ignored the warnings given by the game and walked over the edge of a cliff, falling to his doom. However, MUD1 added a new element—interaction with other humans via the game. In MUD1, not only could the computer kill you, but so could your fellow players. I had forgotten this component until one of my students recently stabbed me in the back (virtually, but fatally) while I demonstrated MUD1 during class.

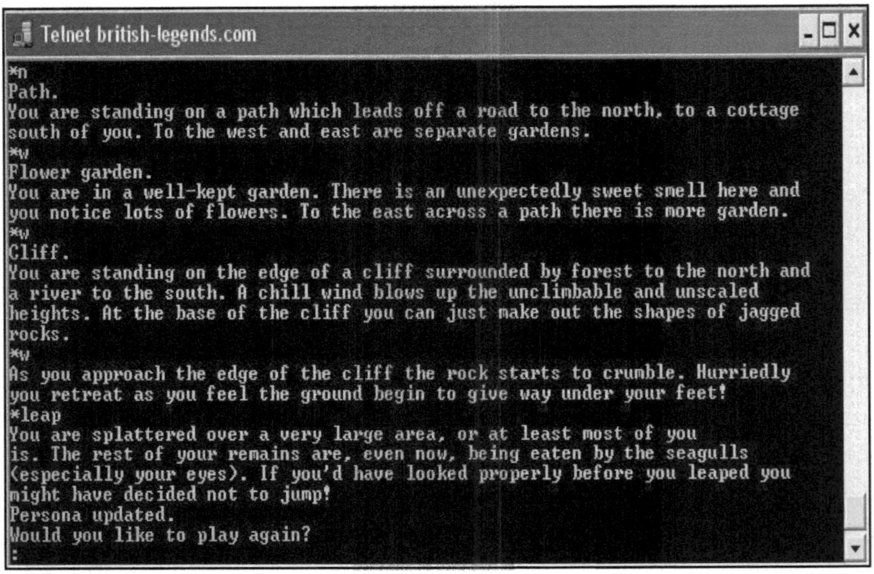

Figure 2.6: MUD1

As seen in the figure, MUD1 (and the earlier Zork and Colossal Cave Adventure) had solely text-based interfaces, with the user typing in commands or chat via the keyboard. Since this was prior to today's mouse interface, knowledge of commands was essential in order to communicate with the program and other users. As seen in Figure 2.6, movement was accomplished by typing directions—in this case w directed the player to go west. This could also be done via the full command go west. In order to talk with other avatars, it was necessary for users to type a double quotation mark (") before their message or they could say something to everyone in the world by using sh (shout) before their message. Since the programming and size of these games was very limited due to the computing power of the day, the number of commands "understood" by the programs was very small, resulting in many messages along the line of "I don't understand that."

As time and technology progressed, MUDs were developed that were considered to be Objected Oriented. These MOOs (MUDs, Object-Oriented) had many of the same characteristics as their predecessors—text-based, multi-user environments—but they added a great flexibility that many educators took advantage of. Unlike MUDs, MOOs allowed for object-oriented programming within the server. This meant that the owner of a MOO could add a new room or object to the environment with relative ease, and without the need to write an entirely new program. These rooms and objects, while still text-based, could serve as educational spaces for users in a way that MUDs could not. While I was a PhD student at the University of Arizona, the Old Pueblo MOO was developed by Professor Roxanne Mountford and her team. Any instructor in the English program could request that a room be added to the MOO, and a number of instructors held online meetings and/or office hours for their students in the space.

As with MUDs, the number of MOOs that are still up and running has diminished very rapidly over the last decade with the advent of VWs and MMORPGs. However, one of the most popular, SchMOOze University (See Figure 2.7), was still up and running at the time of this book.

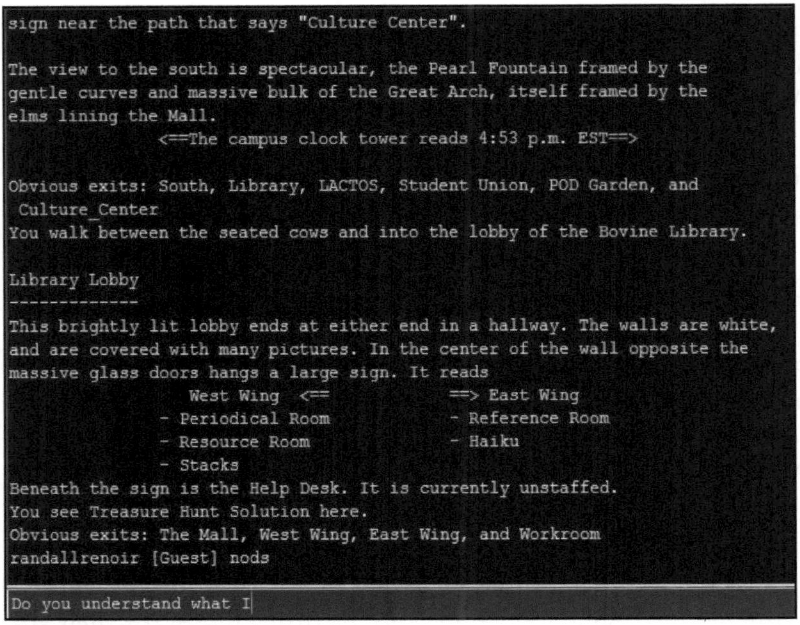

Figure 2.7: SchMOOze University

Habitat

Habitat (see Figure 2.8), released by Lucasfilm in 1986, was the first Virtual World that was both massively multiplayer (though not on the scale of the VWs of today) and used a graphics interface that would seem familiar to the users of today's VWs. Habitat used the power of the new Commodore 64 computer (yes, that is a "massive" 64k of RAM), which had better graphics performance than that of other computers of the time. As seen in Figure 2.8, the message typed by users in the white dialog box at the bottom of the screen showed up above their heads as a dialog bubble. This technique is still used in a number of other VWs today. As seen in the figure, Habitat was 2-D, but did include fully customizable avatars. Unlike in MUDs or MOOs, Habitat users were actually able to see another avatar approach.

However, unlike in later 3-D virtual worlds, an avatar in Habitat was unable to walk "into" the scene to explore the inside of a house like the one seen in the figure. If efforts like PLATO, MUDs, and MOOs are the grandfathers of today's VWs, then Habitat must be seen as a father figure to the VWs discussed below.

Figure 2.8: Habitat Interface

While Habitat most certainly represents a technological leap in the area of VWs, Chip Morningstar and F. Randall Farmer (the co-creators of that environment), found that "people" were the real key to a successful environment.

> The essential lesson that we have abstracted from our experiences with Habitat is that a cyberspace is defined more by the interactions among the actors within it than by the technology with which it is implemented. While we find much of the work presently being done on elaborate interface technologies [...] both exciting and promising, the almost mythical euphoria that currently seems to surround all this hardware is, in our opinion, both excessive and somewhat misplaced. We can't help having a nagging sense that it's all a bit of a distraction from the really pressing issues. At the core of our vision is the idea that cyberspace is necessarily a multiple-participant environment. It seems to us that the things that are important to the inhabitants of such an environment are the capabilities available to them, the characteristics of the other people they encounter there, and the ways these various participants can affect each other. (2001: 173–174)

This, once again, sends an important message to teachers. The tool itself—no matter how advanced the VW—is not the critical feature for telecollaboration. The design of the telecollaboration activities (see Chapter 5) themselves, and the active participation of the students, will either ensure or doom the collaboration.

An Overview of Current Popular Virtual Worlds

Over the last decade, VWs (including all the varieties discussed above) have exploded in popularity. A complete discussion of modern VWs is simply not possible for several reasons. First, new VWs are constantly being developed—and sometimes soon thereafter going out of business. Second, the sheer number of VWs is a bit staggering. The gaming website mmohut <http://mmohut.com/> —which discusses and reviews currently available MMORPGs that are free to play—recently (May 3, 2011) listed 290 MMORPGs, not including ones that have free trials, and also not including many of the VWs discussed later in this chapter, as they do not typically have a heavy role play element. A similar site <http://www.mmorpg.com/> listed 414 games on that same date, and included most of those discussed later in this chapter. An earlier check of the latter site in Feb. 2010 found only 348 games, meaning an increase in games listed of 119%. Neither of these sites shows MMORPGs that are played solely in languages other than English, so the actual number should be much larger.

In addition to the difficulty of determining how many VWs exist, coming up with concrete numbers of users is equally problematic. This is particularly true as one way that players are attracted to a game is by discovering that it is popular (our natural desire to be part of the latest and greatest). Because of this, many VWs have been accused of inflating membership numbers, often by keeping members in their totals lists even if they are no longer active users. Other

VWs have had problems with bots (particularly Second Life) which have been counted as users even though they are empty avatars used only to artificially inflate the popularity of regions within the worlds. In addition, some users have multiple accounts with a VW (I know one user who has seven different SL accounts) or accounts with multiple MMORPGs. Nevertheless, the numbers of users of VWs is staggering. World of Warcraft (see Figure 2.2) is perhaps the best known MMORPG for many of the readers of this book (with over 13 million current users), yet it is dwarfed in user numbers by others, such as the Korean MMORPGs Ragnarok Online (25 million +), Scions of Fate (35 million +), and the child-friendly MapleStory (50 million +).

Although the largest number of users tend towards role play games, the number of users of VWs is also increasing rapidly. KZero, a VW consulting firm, maintains there are now more than 800 million users worldwide (see Figure 2.9) and because KZero does not track MMORPGs, adding those numbers to the total would put the user total at well over 1 billion. However, as mentioned earlier, true user statistics are very difficult to determine. As seen in Figure 2.9, the heaviest users of VWs are in the age group ranging from 10–15, but the most rapidly expanding user group over the course of 2009 were those between 15–25, who increased by over 260% during that time period. Overall, the number of users of VWs doubled over that same time period.

As might be imagined, VWs vary widely in terms of their popularity, their intended audiences, type of graphical interfaces, user controls, themes, appropriate age groups, and a number of other factors. The age factor is increasingly important in Virtual Worlds. From a creator or producer standpoint, VWs have much more competition than just a few years ago, and many VW producers now aim their worlds at a narrow segment of the market rather than aiming for a general audience. As seen in Figure 2.10, one of the most popular VWs is Habbo, which is primarily aimed at the 10–15 year-old age group (KZero).

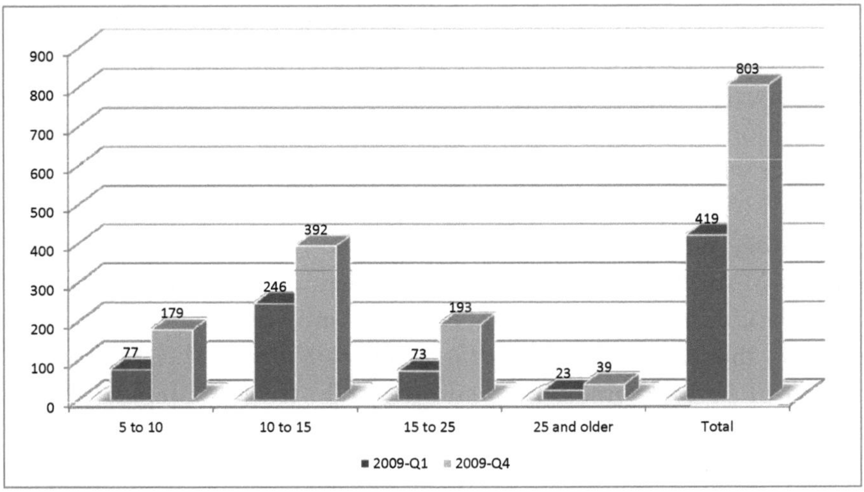

Figure 2.9: Increase in VW Accounts in 2009
<http://www.kzero.co.uk/blog/?p=4028>

In a similar manner to trends in music, movies, and books, younger users of VWs seem to very aware of the age they were created for, and many 12-year olds would not care to be seen hanging around with the "kids" in Webkinz. As discussed later in this book, the age factor is also an important element for those considering using VWs for language teaching since many of the VWs aimed at older audiences are definitely not appropriate for children.

Even though it is not possible to examine even all of the most popular VWs in this book, an overview of some of the most important ones (see Figure 2.11 and below) helps to give a picture of a number of important features, including: how much it costs to use the world, who the intended audience is, the theme of the VW, how many users have subscribed to the world, and how the world may be accessed.

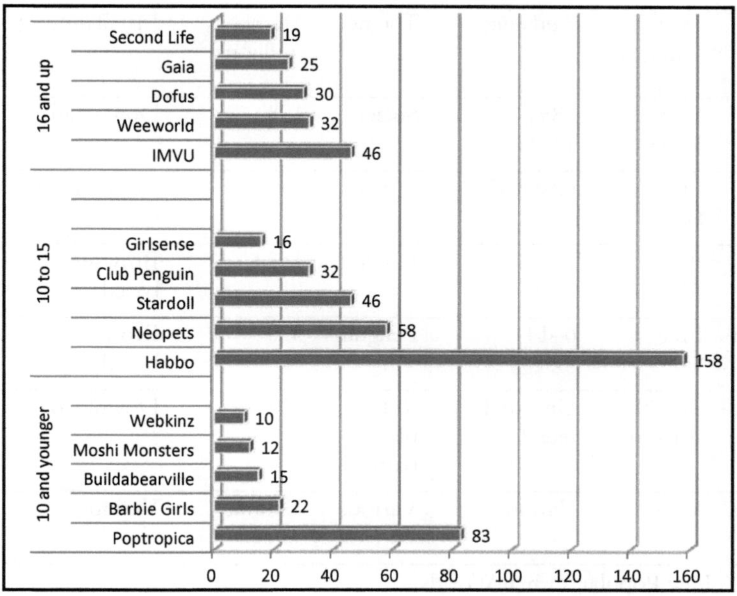

Figure 2.10: Most Popular VWs by Age Group (users in millions) <http://www.kzero.co.uk/blog/?p=4028)>

All of the VWs listed in Figure 2.11, and most VWs in general, allow users to customize their avatars, although the range of these changes varies greatly. Whether the default avatar is a penguin (Club Penguin), a human (Habbo, SL, Active Worlds) or something else (e.g., an Elf in WoW), one of the things that usually differentiates between noobs and more experienced users is how much their avatar has been changed from the default.

In addition, most of these VWs have free accounts, with the paid versions offering extra incentives like game currency. A paid membership in IMVU results in the user receiving 5,000 credits per month that they can buy things with in-world. SL offers 300 Lindens per week and has now begun offering a free home and plot of land to all premium members.

	Cost (/mo)	Audience[3]	Theme	Members (millions)[4]	Installation
Second Life	Free/ $9.95	18+/ 13–17	Social	19+	Download
Active Worlds	Free/ $6.95	unstated	Social	2+	Browser add-on
Habbo	Free/ $4.99	13+	Hotel	158+	Browser-based
Club Penguin	Free/ $5.95	6–14	Penguins	32+	Browser-based
World of Warcraft[5]	$14.99 + software	Unstated, but teen+	Role play, battle	11+	Download
Custom-built worlds	Various	Various	Various	Various	Various

Figure 2.11: A Few Popular Virtual Worlds

Second Life

Second Life (more details in Chapter 4) was launched in 2003 by Linden Labs, created by Philip Rosedale. The SL user system was until recently divided into two primary grids: Second Life, which was only available to users over the age of 18, and Teen Second Life (which closed in December, 2010), aimed at users between 13–17. These two grids have now been combined with teen users having restricted access to the main grid. SL has its own economy, based on the Linden currency, with users having the ability to both buy and sell Lindens for their own RL currency.

3 Based on information from program websites.

4 Member numbers based on data collected on March 23rd, 2010 from program websites and other public sources.

5 Though really a MMORPG, WoW is included here for sake of comparison.

Figure 2.12: Second Life: Edo Japan

SL is often considered to be the Wild West of VWs, partly due to the hand-off philosophy of its creators. This means that the continents and many thousands of private islands in Second Life consist of content that has been primarily created by users of SL. These sims (the name for an individual region in SL) may have any theme, ranging from New York City, to Paris, to Ancient Japan (See Figure 2.12[6]), to a tropical island, etc. Advanced users may sell their own creations either in SL or on the Second Life Marketplace™, which may be thought of as the Amazon.com™ of Second Life. Shopping, both within SL and on Marketplace, is a popular activity for many of the users of this VW.

Communication in SL can be accomplished via text chat (either public chat or private IM), voice chat (also either public or private),

6 In all screenshots from VWs, avatar names are masked or removed (except for the author's or when permission given), any text that might identify users has been removed as well. In some cases (e.g., Club Penguin) both names and all chat has been removed to protect privacy of younger users.

emoticons, and gestures. Unlike some of the VWs discussed below (those aimed at younger teens and children), SL has no restrictions on the language used within the main world. Instead, SL has recently implemented new policies that restrict certain areas of SL to users who have been "age verified."

SL has a very strong community of educators in fields ranging from genetics to language learning, and there are many groups devoted to education in SL. Additional information on Second Life, and its potential for telecollaboration and language learning, may be found in Chapter 4.

Active Worlds

Active Worlds was publicly launched in 1997, and currently consists of 1,000 different worlds, ranging from AWTeen to Zadar. Free users of AW are tourists, and are dressed accordingly (see Figure 2.13, for my Fabioesque European Tourist).

Figure 2.13: Active Worlds: Europe

Citizens have the ability to change their appearance, can create permanent builds within a world, have the potential to purchase their own world, and are given a number of other permissions not available to tourists. The appearance of tourist avatars varies depending on the world in which they are located. This is determined by the owner of that world. While the "standard" tourist outfit consists of a Hawaiian style shirt, as shown in the figure the tourist outfit on the Europe world is quite different.

For communication, AW offers many of the same features as Second Life, including text chat (public and private), voice chat, and gestures. However, while tourists can hear voice chat in AW, they are not able to speak. Active World's policy statement is more restrictive than that of Second Life, both in terms of speech and visuals, in that users are to refrain from:

> Displaying material containing nudity, pornography, or sexual material of a lewd, lecherous or obscene nature and intent or that violate local, state and national laws.
>
> Providing material that is grossly offensive to the online community, including blatant expressions of bigotry, prejudice, racism, hatred or excessive profanity. <http://www.activeworlds.com/community/terms.asp>

As in the case of SL, AW has a strong education component, and this VW has created the Active Worlds Educational Universe (AWEU) in response. This universe currently has more than 80 worlds devoted to education.

Habbo

Habbo (previously called Habbo Hotel) first came online in 2000 in Finland and bills itself as the "world's largest virtual hotel." Each new user is given a basic room in the hotel, and paid subscribers receive 35 Habbo coins and a "rare" piece of furniture a month.

Users can customize and expand their rooms as they accumulate more coins, and they can also open up their room to the public or keep it private. As seen in Figure 2.14, the hotel itself includes a variety of other spaces, such as this waiting lounge, gardens, restaurants, other social areas, and a marketplace where users can buy items for their rooms or avatar.

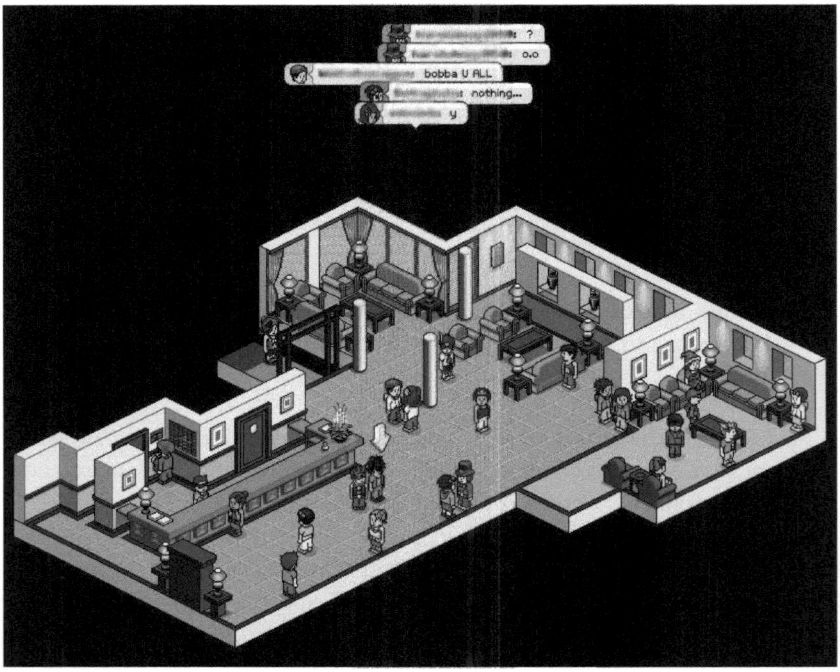

Figure 2.14: Habbo Waiting Lounge

Habbo users are also given their own customizable homepage, and have the ability to embed their hotel room (or other public areas) into another webpage. Movement in Habbo is accomplished by clicking on the area where the user wishes her avatar to go, and the avatar then makes her way to the selected location without further assistance. Unlike many VWs, Habbo is divided into a number of individual communities, largely based on language. As seen in Figure 2.15, there are now 32 Habbo communities around the world, though some of these (e.g., Australia and New Zealand) link to the same hotel. At the current time there is currently nothing like a "shuttle service" to take members between these different communities, but it is possible to log into the Habbo for another country with the appropriate URL.[7] As might be imagined, this has the potential to provide an abundant source of native speakers of a variety of different languages for students seeking practice partners. This VW has no option for voice chat.

Argentina	Australia	Austria	Belgium
Brazil	Canada	Chile	Columbia
Denmark	Ecuador	Finland	France
Germany	Ireland	Italy	Malaysia
Mexico	Netherlands	New Zealand	Norway
Peru	Portugal	Singapore	Spain
Sweden	Switzerland	UK	USA
Venezuela	Morocco	Philippines	Uruguay

Figure 2.15: Habbo Communities

Habbo also has a very strong policy regarding community safety, as laid out in their corporate policy:

> Providing a safe social environment for the users is a top priority in Habbo. In order to keep the community as safe as possible, Habbo uses active moderation, user education and automatic language filtering. Habbo is constantly patrolled by adult moderators who follow the discussions, kick out and ban wrongdoers and help the users with their questions. In Habbo Home users are also provided with an additional reporting tool, which enables them to report inappropriate content to the staff members. <http://www.sulake.com/habbo>

In the case of "swearing and racist or sexist language" those words are eliminated in the visible chat and "bobba" is seen instead. An example of this can be seen in Figure 2.14, where a user tells the room "bobba U ALL."

7 A complete listing of community URLs may be found on the Habbo website: <http://www.sulake.com/habbo>.

Club Penguin

Club Penguin (see Figure 2.16) came online in 2005 and was bought by Disney in 2007. As implied by the name, the avatars in this VW are all penguins. With a paid membership, users can create their own igloo, gather additional outfits and pieces of furniture, and gain access to an increased number of games (and levels) on the site.

Figure 2.16: Club Penguin

As in the case of *Habbo*, one of the primary concerns in this VW is the safety of the participants using it. The site includes no outside advertising and provides live moderation by *Club Penguin* employees. As seen in the top right-hand corner of Figure 2.16, there is always the *Moderator* button available (the shield icon on the screen) so that a user can contact an adult directly for help. In addition, this VW also places two possible limits on the chat that the players can engage in:

> **Ultimate Safe Chat** limits what users can say to a predefined menu of greetings, questions and statements, as well as emotes, actions and greeting cards.

When it comes to chatting, these users can only see other Ultimate Safe Chat Messages.

Standard Safe Chat allows players to type their own messages to other users. Every message is filtered to allow only pre-approved words and phrases, and block attempts to communicate a phone number or other personally identifiable information. <http://www.clubpenguin.com/parents/player_safety. htm>

An example of the Ultimate Safe Chat interface (Figure 2.17) shows how the system works. The user has access to a number of topic headings if they click on the chat button, which may be seen in the lower-left hand corner of the screenshot (the chat bubble). Once a topic heading is selected (hello), a sub-menu appears, etc. In this instance, selecting "How are you doing?" would result in that message appearing in the public chat area. Responses may also be accessed via this menu, starting with the "answers" option.

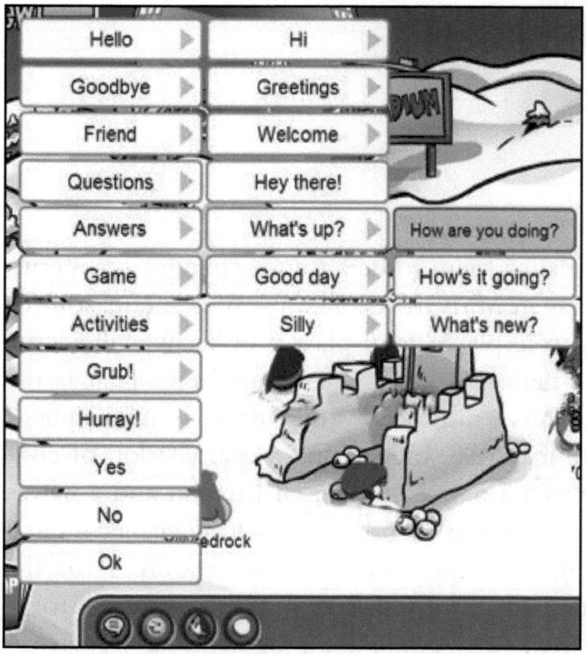

Figure 2.17: Ultimate Safe Chat

Club Penguin does not have an option for voice chat, but there is a standard set of emoticons available to all players. This VW also has a weekly newspaper, *The Club Penguin Times*, with news, user-submitted questions, an advice column, and more.

World of Warcraft

World of Warcraft (shown in Figure 2.2) shares all of the common features that define VWs in general, but as implied in the acronym, this MMORPG adds the key element of role play—in this case war roleplay.

- On-line 3D environment.
- Avatars.
- Real-time Interactivity.
- 24-hour Accessibility.
- Persistence.
- Social Space.
- Numbers.
- Role Play.

While this may at first glance seem to be a minor change, it is a critical one since the role play in MMORPGs like WoW is the reason for their existence. A good role player (and player) in WoW will accrue more skills, more gold, better weapons, "level up," etc. That is the purpose of the game. This is not to say that there is no language learning that takes place in WoW. Indeed, in an examination of conversation in WoW between a native speaker of Russian and a native speaker of English, Steve Thorne found parallels to what occurs in a RL classroom, including "drawing from external resources for the production of experimental L2 production [...]," a "request for a comprehension check [...]," an "evaluative judgment," a "repair sequence," and an "overt correction" (Thorne, 2008: 321). Given this type of interaction and the international nature of online gaming, there can be no doubt that MMORPGs are sites of tremendous amounts of language practice and cultural exchange.

Custom-built worlds/SIEs

All of the VWs discussed up to this point are available to anyone (at least those that still exist) and were created as commercial products (at least all the modern VWs). However there is another important segment to the universe of VWs, sometimes referred to as *Synthetic Immersive Environments* (SIEs), which are "designed to target educational objectives through the creation of a meaningful collaborative space in which the participants are directly engaged in activity related to specific domains of knowledge" (Thorne, Black, & Sykes, 2009: 812). These share many of the same characteristics as VWs and MMORPGs, with the possible exception of numbers.

SIEs, as mentioned above, are carefully designed environments that often have a very specific educational purpose. Many who grew up in the United States are no doubt familiar with Oregon Trail, a game that was often used in high school computer labs (see Figure 2.18).

Figure 2.18: Oregon Trail

In this game a group of students (typically 5) had to guide their wagon along the Oregon Trail. Along the way, there were historical lessons about the trail and, no doubt, at least one or two members of the party were lost to starvation or dysentery. While not a true SIE in the modern sense (not 3D, not a social space, etc.) this type of game is the forefather of the modern SIE.

Modern SIEs share some of these features of games like Oregon Trail, but add the true interactivity, 3D environment, accessibility, and social space of VWs. One example of this type of SIE is Croquelandia (see Figure 2.19).

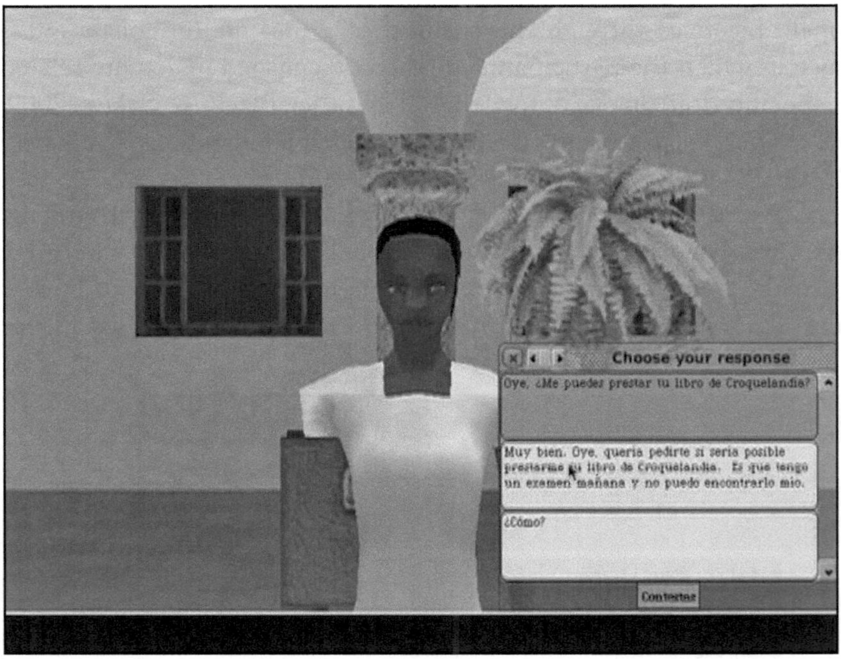

Figure 2.19: Croquelandia

The creators of Croquelandia (see Sykes, 2008 for a discussion of this SIE and her research there) used Croquet, an open-source program designed to allow users to create "deeply collaborative multi-user online virtual world applications on and across multiple operating systems and devices" <http://www.opencroquet.org/index.php/

Main_Page>. Rather than creating an entire VW or universe, an SIE typically consists of a smaller, controlled environment. In Croquelandia, this is a market in a Spanish-speaking town where the students can interact with programmed sellers as seen in Figure 2.19.

While the use of a program like Croquet requires "experienced software developers" (ibid), there are other SIEs that make use of existing VWs. For example, Quest Atlantis <http://atlantis.crlt.indiana.edu/> makes use of the Active Worlds system to create SIEs focused on educational activities, ranging from statistics, to Frankenstein, to issues related to water quality. Other educators are engaging in similar projects using Second Life. MMORPGs and SIEs can both certainly play important roles in the education process, but they will not be focused on heavily in this text since they are both certainly worthy of their own books.

Summary

As mentioned earlier in this chapter, there are an enormous number of VWs available online, all of which offer many opportunities for telecollaboration. This chapter covered a few of the most popular, but is in no way meant to be a comprehensive overview of currently available VWs—as indicated in this chapter, these are quite numerous and constantly changing. However, this chapter does provide a history of the field and a sample of VWs (and other online games) that are potentially useful to language educators. This topic will be explored in much greater detail in Chapter 4 and beyond in this text.

Suggested Readings

Print Resources

Edlinger, M. (2008). *Interaction in virtual worlds: Concepts, applications, and restrictions*. Saarbrücken: VDM.

Kapp, M. & O'Driscoll, T. (2010). *Learning in 3D: Adding a new dimension to enterprise learning and collaboration.* San Francisco: Pfeiffer.

Web-based Resources

Silberman, S. (1997). *Physics in the 1960s: PLATOFest*: Retrieved December 8, 2010 from <http://physics. illinois.edu/history /PLATOfest.asp>.

Active Worlds. Retrieved September 14, 2011 from <http://www. activeworlds.com/>.

British Legends: Site for MUD1. Retrieved September 14, 2011 from <http://www.british-legends. com/>.

Club Penguin. Retrieved September 14, 2011 from <http:// www.clubpenguin.com/>.

Cyber1: A group dedicated to the preservation of PLATO. Retrieved March 2, 2011 from <http://www.cyber1.org/>.

Habbo. Retrieved September 14, 2011 from <http://www.habbo. com/>.

SchMOOze University. Retrieved May 2, 2011 from <http:// schmooze.hunter.cuny.edu/> (hoping it is still there!).

Second Life. Retrieved May 2, 2011 from <http://www.secondlife .com>.

World of Warcraft: Retrieved May 7, 2011 from <http://www. worldofwarcraft.com/index.xml>.

Chapter 3: Virtual Worlds, Learning, and Theory

> The correct path had the aspect of a narrow row of stones cutting through a grayish-green swamp [...]. The subconscious knew what the stones represented, handled the chaining of routines from one information net to another, but it was the conscious mind of the skilled traveler that must make the decisions [...]. (Vernor Vinge, True Names, 1986)

Introduction

Why should we use Virtual Worlds for language teaching, and more specifically for telecollaborative language learning? Because they are fun? Because they do something for our students? Because they enable situations for collaborative learning? Because they will help in the language learning process? One would hope that the answer to all of these questions is yes, but it is important that we understand exactly why VWs may be useful in the language learning process. Just as in the novel Portal, we must not rely solely on what our subconscious minds tell about the potential for VWs and the path we should take in using them for language learning (that is likely only the fun part of our brain speaking). Instead, it is necessary for our conscious minds to explore the rationale for their use...or non use. This is where learning theory is key. Accordingly, this chapter will first examine a number of learning theories that apply to VWs and telecollaboration, and then look at some of the existing research into the effect of CMC and VWs on language learning in order to provide firmer answers to the questions posed above.

Virtual Worlds and Theory

There is no Theory for Virtual Worlds and Language Learning. This does not mean that there are no theories that may be applied to this field, but, rather that there is no single theory that has been created specifically with VWs in mind. I would argue that perhaps no such Theory is necessary since learning in VWs is still learning rather than some radically new process. The theories and methodologies (or at least some of them) that apply to language acquisition, language learning, and language teaching in the real world may also be applied to virtual worlds, provided that they are relevant. This chapter will provide an overview of some of the existing theories that help to illustrate how VWs may be useful in the language learning process.

A complete overview of all the theories related to language learning that might apply to Virtual Worlds is beyond the scope of this text. Indeed, it could certainly be argued that any book that has been written on language learning theory will include at least some discussion of theories that might potentially be applied to these environments. The theories discussed in this chapter include some of those most pertinent and/or cited in the field of CMCLL and VWLL, including:

- Experiential Education (Dewey)
- Zone of Proximal Development (Vygotsky)
- Experiential Learning (Kolb)
- Interaction Hypothesis (Long, 1980, 1981)

Ironically, some of these ideas were first proposed long before the invention of Computer-Mediated Communication and Virtual Worlds, before the creation of the Internet (or even computer networks), and even before the creation of modern computers. All of these theories emphasize, in some way, the importance of interaction and collaboration in the learning process—something that VWs are ideally suited for (as will be demonstrated in the second half of this book).

Experiential Education (Dewey)

John Dewey (1859–1952, see Figure 3.1) was perhaps the greatest proponent of progressive education at the beginning of the 20th century and also a key figure and founder of the concept of *Experiential Education.* While he was the author of a tremendous number of articles and books over the course of his sixty-eight year academic career, two of his best know best known books are *Democracy and Education* (1916) and *Experience and Education* (1939). His views in both of these texts contain potential applications to the use of Virtual Worlds for language learning.

Figure 3.1: John Dewey

In many of his works, and certainly in the two mentioned above, Dewey was highly critical of the "traditional" schools of his time which seemed to be very separate from the real world. However, in his descriptions of such schools, I think that many of us will find an environment that is still quite familiar today, with "[...] the ordinary schoolroom, its time-schedules, schemes of classification, of examination and promotion, and rules of order [...]" (1939: 2). He also found that in such traditional schools, the students were far too passive, the books far too important, and the teachers too much in the front and center:

> [In a traditional school] the attitude of pupils must, upon the whole, be one of docility, receptivity, and obedience. Books, especially textbooks, are the chief representatives of the lore and wisdom of the past, while teachers are the organs through which pupils are brought into effective connection with the material. Teachers are the agents through which knowledge and skills are communicated and rules of conduct enforced. (p. 3)

This criticism of the traditional schools of 1939 may certainly be applied to many language classrooms that exist today, where the textbook (often a comprehensive textbook being the primary—or sole—printed resource used in the class) and teacher are the center of the classroom. While I have found this to be particularly true of many of teachers I've worked with from some locations outside of the U.S. or Europe, it also brings to mind my own student teaching (1990, in the field of history) where I was told to only use the materials from the textbook, and the model given by the master teacher consisted of having the students read from the textbook during class time since she wanted to be sure the students were doing the readings.

For Dewey, a progressive school stood in opposition to the tenets of traditional schools in fundamental ways:

> To imposition from above is opposed expression and cultivation of individuality; to external discipline is opposed free activity; to learning from texts and teachers, learning through experience; to acquisition of isolated skills and techniques by drill, is opposed acquisition of them as means of attaining ends which make direct vital appeal; to preparation for a more or less remote future is opposed making the most of the opportunities of present life; to static aims and materials is opposed acquaintance with a changing world. (1939: 5–6)

While the student in the traditional school is primarily passive, gaining knowledge passed down via the teacher and book, the student in the progressive school is both an active and a passive individual who learns by doing and who learns things that she can apply at the present time. These students are active in that they try things and then, based on that experience, they "suffer or undergo the consequences" (1916: 163). These consequences (whether positive or negative) are a key part of the learning process.

This is not to say that the teacher no longer plays an important role in the progressive school. Indeed, in many ways the role of teacher is even more important since the quality (1939: 16) of the experience for the students is critical. Though this work predates terms like "teacher-centered" and "student-centered," Dewey saw the position of the progressive teacher as changing from "the position of external boss or dictator but [taking] on that of leader of group activities" (p. 66). A student in a progressive school was not free to do whatever he liked. Indeed, Dewey was very critical of some schools that called themselves progressive and seemed to take this stance.

Since students in true progressive schools would have contact with both the teacher and also additional contacts (usually adult) outside of the classroom, they would actually receive more guidance than students in a traditional school.

A progressive classroom is no longer totally reliant on the book or the traditional role of the teacher, so the teacher is now instead responsible for deciding "the kinds of materials, of methods, and of social relationships that are appropriate to the new education" (p. 19). The teacher must also become aware of the new educational environment, which may (and should) include places and people not connected to the traditional school since this new environment will be an important new source of education for the students. For example, this might include the use of a builder to teach the students about geometry rather than the traditional geometry textbook. However, it was not enough for a progressive teacher to merely provide experiences for her students since not all experiences are created equal and some can even be considered to be "mis-educative" (p. 13).

Experiences should be enjoyable for the students and also provide them with the opportunity to learn.

Two key and interrelated concepts for Experiential Education are *situation* and *interaction*. The situation is the environment in which interaction takes place, while the interaction might be between a teacher and student, students working in a group, or it might even be between the student and a book or a machine (e.g., something in a factory). According to Dewey, this interaction need not even take place in the real world at all, since "[even] when a person builds a castle in the air he is interactive with the objects which he constructs in fancy" (p. 42). Ironically enough, this was long before we did have the ability to build a castle in the sky, albeit in Second Life (see Figure 3.2). (More on castle building in later chapters.) Although O'Dowd (2006), defined telecollaboration as a way "to connect language learners in different countries for the development of collaborative project work and intercultural exchange" (p. 9), Experiential Education saw this collaboration (interaction) as taking place in some shared location—again, likely due to a lack of potential for distance learning at that time. VWs provide a key linking component between Experiential Education and Telecollaboration in that a VW can provide that shared situation for the learners' avatars, even if their corporeal selves are located many miles apart.

In Dewey's progressive model interaction can make use of play since "play and work correspond, point for point, with the traits of the initial stage of knowing, which consists [...] in learning how to do things and in acquaintance with things and processes gained in the doing" (1916: 229). If students can learn by playing, then the educational goal is still achieved.

Figure 3.2: Castle in the Virtual Sky

Although computers and VWs would have been only constructions of fancy in John Dewey's day, and anything "tele" (except perhaps for the telegraph and telephone) would not have been available, Dewey's theories have strong implications for the use of VWs for telecollaboration. As mentioned in the previous chapters, VWs are social environments and sites of tremendous interaction amongst many thousands of users on a daily basis. For an educator following the tenets of Experiential Education today, making use of a VW as the *situation* is perfectly appropriate since a variety of types of interaction (collaborations) may take place there.

This interaction might be between a teacher and student (with those individuals located in the same computer lab in RL or thousands of miles apart), students working in a group, or between the students and some machine within that VW. In the case of the students working in a group, the VW may be used for telecollaboration activities ranging from a cultural exchange between two classes of students (e.g., one located in Spain and one in the U.S.), students working in small groups to create artwork within a VW, or to just get together for play. For Dewey, Experiential Education was about getting students outside of the traditional classroom to provide them with expanded opportunities for interactions. VWs provide an ideal situation for such collaboration.

Zone of Proximal Development (Vygotsky)

When I recently assigned a reading by Lev Vygotsky (1896–1934, see Figure 3.3) to my students taking a seminar on Virtual Worlds and Language Learning, I was surprised when—during class discussion—one of them asked if I had ever had the chance to meet Vygotsky. Needless to say (note the date of Vygotsky's death!), I found this question to be disturbing on multiple levels. As it turned out, this student (and others) was confused by the fact that most of Vygotsky's works were first published in English in the late 1970s (resulting in an English copyright from that decade), and they did not realize that Vygotsky was already dead long before the birth of their esteemed professor.

Figure 3.3: Vygotsky

Whatever the dates of his writing, there can be little doubt that Vygotsky's works, and in particular *Mind in Society: The Development of Higher Mental Processes* (1978), have had a significant impact on research into CMC, Telecollaboration, and VWs and language learning, with a number of authors in those areas referring to his theories of learning (e.g., Dooly, 2010; Steinkuehler, 2004; Bronack, Riedl, & Tashner, 2006; Price & Rogers, 2004; Dickey, 2005; Bystrom & Barfield, 1999; Bricken, 1991; Barab, Hay, Barnet & Squire, 2001; Molka-Danielsen, 2009; Broadribb, Peachey, Carter, & Westrap, 2009).

Perhaps the best known concept from *Mind in Society* is the Zone of Proximal Development (ZPD). According to Vygotsky, this (see Figure 3.4) is "the distance between the actual developmental level as determined by independent problem solving and the level of potential development as determined through problem solving under adult guidance or in collaboration with more capable peers" (1978: 86).

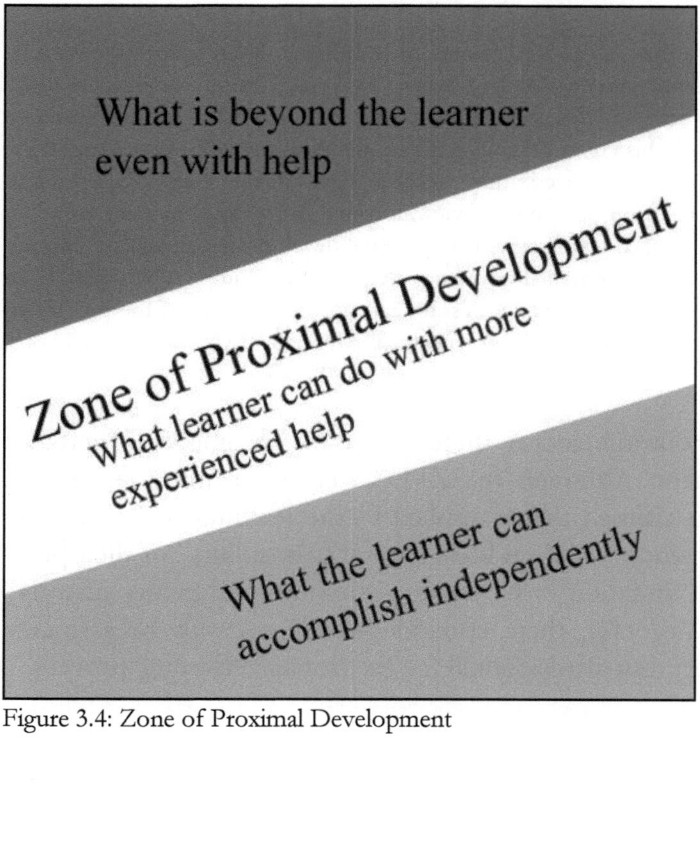

Figure 3.4: Zone of Proximal Development

For Vygotsky, this notion of the ZPD is critical since he maintains that "human learning presupposes a specific social nature and a process by which children grow into the intellectual life of those around them" (p. 88). Because learning is inherently social, and because children are often around people who are more experienced, this means that "children are [therefore] capable of doing much more in collective activity" (p. 88).

The significance of the ZPD for learners is that this is the zone where the functions which take place (whether related to social rules, cultural knowledge, language, or anything else) "[...] have not yet matured but are in the process of maturation, functions that will mature tomorrow but are currently in an embryonic state" (p. 86). This importance of the group and social learning goes beyond letting learners accomplish more than they could on their own in a single activity or communicative event. According to Vygotsky, the ZPD is essential for development in general:

> We propose that an essential feature of learning is that it creates the zone of proximal development; that is, learning awakens a variety of internal developmental processes that are able to operate only when the child is interacting with people in his environment and in cooperation with his peers. Once these processes are internalized, they become part of the child's independent achievement. From this point of view, learning is not development; however, properly organized learning results in mental development and sets in motion a variety of developmental processes that would be impossible apart from learning., Thus, learning is a necessary and universal aspect of the process of developing culturally organized, specifically human, psychological functions. (p. 90)

In short, without interaction, there can be no learning, and therefore no development. Although the ZPD refers to learning in general, Vygotsky also claimed that it applied to the learning of language in the same way since "children learn speech from adults" or their peers often through imitation or by "asking questions and giving answers" (p. 84). For Vygotsky, then, imitation would not only be a sincere form of flattery, but also essential for the language learning process.

One of the most problematic issues for language learners in the past has been how to access those more knowledgeable individuals that Vygotsky maintains are essential in the learning process. For a student studying English in a rural region of Venezuela in the 1970s, interaction with a native speaker of English (a more knowledgeable individual, one would hope) would have been very difficult, if not impossible. However, in today's world, CMC tools such as VWs give learners potential access to such individuals from around the world. In some environments, such as the Venezuelan case mentioned above, these tools may still provide learners with their only access to native speakers of the language they wish to study. This access to "more capable peers," in this case either individuals from the culture of interest and/or native speakers of the language being studied, is a key strength of VWs that will be discussed in more detail in Chapter 5.

As with Dewey, the concept of play is important for Vygotsky. When children play, particularly in imaginary situations, this "teaches the child to guide her behavior not only by immediate perception of objects or by the situation immediately affecting her but also by the meaning of the situation" (p. 97). For preschool children this is when thought and action become important and imagination becomes an important part of the learning process—for example when "a piece of wood begins to be a doll and a stick becomes a horse" (p. 97). Play allows children (or students) to spontaneously practice activities or speech without the need to focus deeply on the meaning. This too can be part of the ZPD, especially if the student is playing with more experienced participants or adults.

Just as in the RW, play can take on a very important role during collaborative exchanges in VWs. I took the recommendations of Dewey and Vygotsky into account during my own design of a group of islands in Second Life focused on education (EduNation Islands: <http://edunation-islands.wikispaces.com/>) because it had also been my experience that play-focused activities in VWs resulted in a great deal of communication between the participants, whatever their levels. This resulted in the inclusion of activities on the island ranging from scuba diving, to boating, hang-gliding, go-kart racing, and many others. While none of these activities fit into the traditional classroom, they all result in increases in language production and communication between the VW collaborators—results that both Vygotsky and Dewey would approve of.

Once again, another old theory may be directly applied to some very new technologies. With Vygotsksy's emphasis on—or perhaps insistence upon—the social nature of learning, telecollaboration via a VW offers a myriad of opportunities for learning to take place in ways that were simply not possible before. Using the tool of the VW, students can engage in a wide variety of cooperative activities (see some samples in Chapter 5) that they cannot accomplish on their own.

Experiential Learning (Kolb)

As might be inferred by the name of the theory, David Kolb (1939–) was heavily influenced by Dewey's theory of experiential education, but also by Lewin's (1951) experiential learning model and by Piaget's work on cognitive development (1970). For Kolb, experiential learning is based on the following premises:

- Learning is best conceived as a process, not in terms of outcomes.
- Learning is a continuous process grounded in experience.
- The process of learning requires the resolution of conflicts between dialectically opposed modes of adaptation to the world.
- Learning is a holistic process of adaptation to the world.
- Learning involves transactions between the person and the environment.
- Learning is the process of creating knowledge. (1984: 26–38)

As with the earlier works discussed above, Kolb's theory sees learning as a process that takes place between the learner and the environment. The individual, especially after the initial stages of the learning process, is not a passive receptor of knowledge. Rather, he is an active member of the learning process via his interaction with the environment.

This idea is often represented as 4-stage model of learning (see Figure 3.5, from Kolb, 1984: 21) which originated in the work of Lewin (1951). In this model, the idea of concrete experience is key, just as it was in Dewey's work:

> Immediate personal experience is the focal point for learning, giving life, texture, and subjective personal meaning to abstract concepts and at the same time providing a concrete, publicly shared reference point for testing the implications and validity of ideas created during the learning process. When human beings share an experience, they can share it fully, concretely, and abstractly. (p. 21)

After engaging in a concrete experience, a learner can then engage in observation and reflection on that experience which, it is hoped, will then lead to the formation of generalizations based on the experience and reflection. Once a new generalization is formed, the learner can then test it in a new situation, via another concrete experience. As this cycle continues, new observations are made, new concepts are added, etc. However, without the concrete experience that is central to this model, the experiential learning process would simply not be possible.

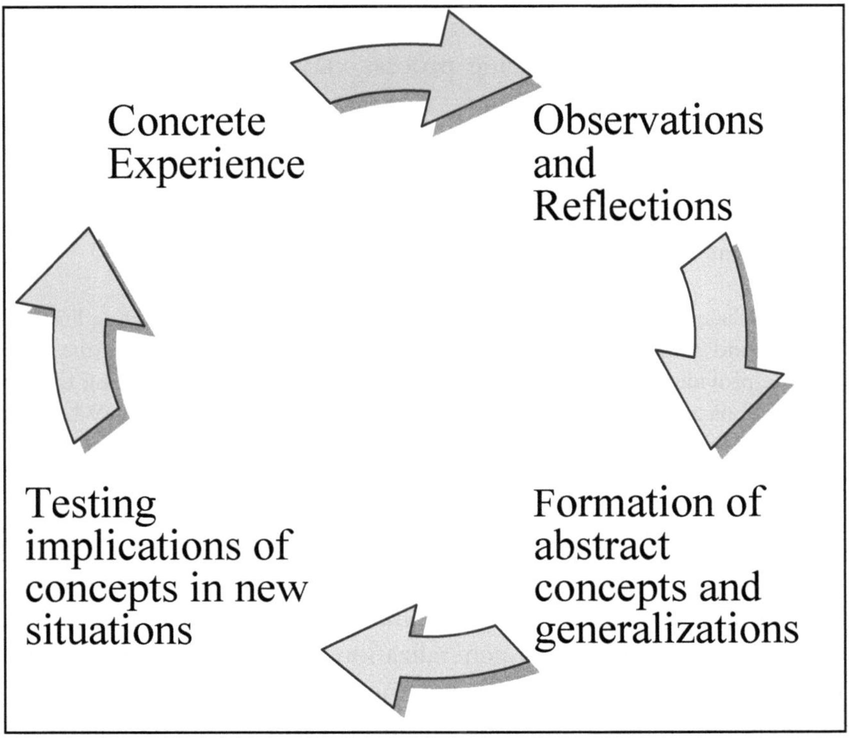

Figure 3.5: Experiential Learning Model (based on Kolb, 1984)

For a language learner utilizing a Virtual World, this concrete experience might take the form of the learner interacting with an individual they encountered in that world (e.g., someone they are working with to build a virtual house). Based on the interaction and communication that takes place during that encounter (e.g., the use of a number of terms related to building something in a VW, watching their partner manipulate different shapes, colors, and textures), the learner could observe how their partner used the language being studied when referring to the shapes, building process, etc. Based on this reflection, the learner may then form generalizations about how language should be used in this type of situation, so that they can then test out these new generalizations when they meet again to continue the interaction.

Interaction Hypothesis (Long, 1980, 1981)

In 1981 Michael Long reviewed 30 studies related to the topic of foreigner talk in order to determine what patterns might exist in their data relating to factors which would facilitate second language acquisition (SLA). Specifically, he looked at the issues of modified input and modified interaction and how these two elements enhanced or detracted from language learning. Based on his examination of the studies he verified the following propositions:

- SLA is possible with unmodified input but modified interaction
- Modified interaction with unmodified input facilitates SLA
- SLA is possible with modified input and modified interaction
- Modified input and modified interaction together facilitate SLA. (1981: 273–274)

In the case of language learners, modified input refers to the use of foreigner talk or teacher talk (both describe simplified speech) when providing input to a language learner, while modified interaction describes "a variety of devices presumably intended to facilitate comprehensions and participation by [...] NNS" (p. 264). According to Long, this could include a wide variety of elements such as repetition of the NNSs utterance, the use of rhetorical questions, etc. The four propositions shown above may be condensed down to two key points for Long:

1. Comprehensible Input, is a requirement for SLA to take place.
2. Modifying the interaction by which that input takes place can help to make input more comprehensible.

Ellis (1991), influenced by Long's work and also by Pica's (1987) extension on the Interaction Hypothesis, adds an additional two-part item:

3.a. Tasks in which there is a need for the participants to exchange information with each other promote more interactional structuring.

3.b. A situation in which the conversational partners share a symmetrical role relationship affords more opportunities for interactional restructuring. (Ellis, 1991: 9)

The addition of Ellis' third item is crucial because it suggests that comprehensible input is more likely to occur in situations where an exchange of information is part of the task and that real exchange is less likely to occur in situations where one partner is much higher or lower in status than the partner. In this case, the status of the teacher would be considered higher than the student, therefore hindering the exchange. The student is more likely to become a listener rather than an active participant.

For educators using VWs, this hypothesis has several important ramifications. First, it suggests to us that if we wish for our students to gain comprehensible input then it may be necessary to help them find the right setting to get the right type of linguistic input. While it may be tempting to simply set our students free in a VW, they—especially lower level students—may have difficulty finding input that is comprehensible for them, or they may find types of input that we would prefer they avoid! Second, it suggests that the activities that take place in those environments should be both interactive and symmetrical in design.

The four sets of theories outlined above were all devised long before the popular VWs of today were ever created. However, the ideas presented in each of these theories helps us to have a clearer understand of why collaboration in VWs can be theoretically relevant for individuals who wish to improve their language skills today.

CMC, Virtual Worlds, and Learning

Investigation into the role of Virtual Worlds in the language acquisition process is still in its infancy, yet there is an existing body of research on related CMC technologies and their effects on language learning. In addition, there is a rapidly increasing amount of research taking place in VWs. While the developing role of CMC and Virtual Worlds in the language learning and teaching process is still an educational work in progress, there is no doubt that computers—and Virtual Worlds in general—are playing an increasingly important role in today's language classrooms

Although some educators or language learners may see little value in the use of CMC and Virtual Worlds in the language learning process, it is quite clear that the students of today are living technological lives, with a great deal of their communication taking place in manners other than face-to-face. This also holds true after completion of school, where "e-mail is now surpassing face-to-face and telephone conversation as the most frequently used communication tool [...]" (Shetzer & Warschauer, 2000: 171). Of course, with the rapid changes in technology, and equally rapid changes in the use of that technology, it should not come as a shock to find that only four years after the quotation above, a study in Korea found that approximately two-thirds of middle and high school students who were polled for a survey on technology use mentioned that they now rarely or never used email. For these students, email was already "an old and formal communication means," and they much preferred to use instant messaging, either via computer or cell phone, rather than waiting for the slow pace of old fashioned email messages (Ki-hong, 2004). If, like me, you are someone who recalls writing actual letters on paper using a pen or pencil which were then delivered in a non-electronic manner, this new focus on instant communication may seem like a strange new world. However, the important point is that this is the communication of the students of today.

As discussed in Chapter 2, since the days of PLATO—and largely due to the foundations created by PLATO—there has been an explosion in the creation and use of both asynchronous and synchronous tools for communication. This trend has also benefitted from the rapid expansion of broadband Internet connections around the world. These tools, ranging from email (for the old fashioned students), to message boards, to blogs, wikis, social networks, VWs, etc., are now used as a natural part of today's communication environment, with many students seemingly spending more time with their fingers flying across their phones sending IMs than actually talking face-to-face.

Research on CMC

In "Language and the Internet," David Crystal (2001: 28) refers to the language being used in CMC communication as Netspeech, which is "a form of communication [...] [that] relies on characteristics belonging to both sides of the speech/writing divide." While some may see netspeech as the end of grammatical language as we know it (a claim that seems to be made about the language of every new generation, beginning long before the invention of the Internet), in actuality it is simply a new method of communication which continues to evolve. In essence, we have now come to a stage when CMC communities have become discourse communities in their own merit—places where Vygotsky's Zone of Proximal Development is valid not just within a single classroom, but for individuals collaborating across the world.

While it is abundantly clear that students today are making use of a number of CMC technologies, perhaps a more important question is whether they should be used as part of the language learning process. As anyone who has learned a second language—especially in a classroom environment—will recall, anxiety and embarrassment seem to be natural parts of the language learning process. From a learner's perspective, as proposed by Stephen Krashen (1985), this anxiety may have the effect of raising the individual's affective filter, making the acquisition of the new language even more difficult. Some research has found that CMC can provide potentially less stressful means of learner-to-learner or learner-to-teacher communication within language classrooms than face-to-face interaction, resulting in additional communication (Fanderclai, 1995; Harris, 1995; Kelm, 1996; Reid, 1994). Sullivan and Pratt's (1996) study quantifies this result, showing full student participation in electronic discourse as compared to 50% participation in face-to-face interaction. This is not to say that CMC necessarily results in a lower quality of discussion. Warschauer (1996) reports that the electronic discussions from his research involved significantly more complex sentence structures than those produced in face-to-face discussions.

Another major advantage that is in keeping with the theories discussed earlier in the chapter is that CMC can extend the interaction possibilities "beyond [the] time constraints and the usual limited circle of interlocutors of classroom pair and group work" (Belcher, 1999: 255). This aspect of convenience is often cited as being an important advantage of CMC for classroom communication, as it enables participants to collaborate outside of the classroom on their own time (Egbert et al., 1999; Snookes, 1995). Research in second language classrooms indicates that networked computers can indeed enhance motivation (Hofsøy, 2001; Paver, 2003; Samsonov, 2001; Warschauer, 1996) and increase self-confidence (Beauvois & Eledge, 1995 Winter & 1996 Spring; Ware, 2004). CMC also provides opportunities for authentic interaction and meaning negotiation (Kern, 1995; Smith, 2003) that are not typically available in a traditional classroom. In ESL/EFL writing classes, other research has shown that the use of CMC enhanced students' confidence in writing and increased quantity in both peer and teacher feedback (Braine, 1997).

Other research has examined how the use of CMC tools can improve sociolinguistic proficiency (Belz & Kinginger, 2002, 2003; Chun, 1994; Kern, 1995; Meskill & Anthony, 2005; Pellettieri, 2000); and how it may help to create a more equal environment for students in multilinguistic, multicultural classrooms (Rheingold, 1993; Sproull

& Kieller, 1991), thus empowering minority students or nonnative English-speaking students in composition classrooms with linguistically and culturally diverse backgrounds (Belcher, 1999). These findings are also seen in Warschauer's (1996) study, which found more equal conversations in CMC in comparison to face-to-face communication, with the normally less vocal students participating more, perhaps because CMC provides "a less threatening means to communicate" (p. 31).

Research on Virtual Worlds

While still in its infancy, with the majority of research on the topic accomplished after 2000, there are an increasing number of articles and books being written on the effect of Virtual Worlds on learning. While many of these efforts look at the more general category of learning rather than specifically focusing on language acquisition, their findings still have important implication for educators in this area. In particular, two recently edited volumes (complete citation in the suggested readings for this chapter), Higher Education in Virtual Worlds: Teaching and Learning in Second Life (Molka-Danielsen & Deutschmann, 2009) and Learning and Teaching in the Virtual World of Second Life (Wankel & Kingsley, 2009) have greatly helped to expand the presentation of research in the field.

In keeping with the wider research on CMC, a number of scholars have looked at the issue of anxiety and learning in VWs. Childress and Braswell (2006) found that students sometimes prefer such online settings because it "allows them time to more completely formulate their thoughts as they respond to the class discussion. Virtual online worlds provide an additional level of personality that is missing from the typical chat room environment" (p. 188). Others found that using an avatar was helpful in that it allowed the participants "to experiment with new and powerful identities" (Shaffer, Squire, Halverson, & Gee, 2004: 6), and that it helped to "loosen them up a bit [...]" (Love, Ross, & Wilhelm, 2009: 68). The fact that VWs have an aspect of play built into the technology also helps to reduce student anxiety. In their study of the VW There (sadly, now gone), Brown and Bell found that the environment "[allowed] communities of players to form who exchange new activities and forms of play with each other" (2004: 357). These findings are echoed by Sant (2009), who examined performance in SL, ranging from music to live art, Roussou (2004) who also examined play in VWs, and by McAleer, Balkun, Zedek, and Trotta (2009) who examined literary analysis in SL as a form of serious play. As implied by the study above, in a VW it is often the case that students are not simply "active, but also actors" (Dillenbourg, Schneider, & Syntenta, 2002: 6). Even researchers from the business world have investigated this component of VWs since it is "difficult to teach students how to think 'outside the box' in a traditional face-to-face or online learning environment" (Love, Ross, & Wilhelm, 2009: 67–68). Learners' sense of anxiety is also lessened over time in VWs because of the sense of community that they encourage in a manner similar to a traditional classroom:

> Students can observe the actions of other students, watch how others interact with the various elements found in the virtual world, and introduce a visual element of proximity which is not available in a typical online classroom. (Childress & Braswell, 2006: 191)

This sense of community is much more difficult to foster in a non-VW online course where students only communicate via forums or email.

A fair amount of the research into learning in VWs has focused on the collaborative nature of these environments (e.g., Churchill & Snowdon, 1998; Dillenbourg, Schneider, & Syntenta, 2002; Brown & Bell, 2004; Price & Rogers, 2004; Roussou, 2004; Shaffer, Squire, Halverson, & Gee, 2004; Gronstedt, 2007; Skiba, 2007; Ball & Pearce, 2009; Bani, Genovesi, Ciregia, Piscioneri, Rapisarda, Salvatori, & Simi, 2009). According to Gronstedt, Second Life is essentially a "social networking tool" which by its very nature encourages collaboration (p. 46). Brown and Bell also maintain that VWs—in this case There—are collaborative due to their nature as social settings build around objects, a point also made by Dickey (2005) regarding Active Worlds. Another reason that collaboration is an important element in VWs is because it is the primary way that new members learn about the environment. By working with more experienced users, the new participants can accomplish more in comparison to working alone. This Vygotskian principle was confirmed by Bystrom & Barfield (1999), who found that students in their VW study were able to complete tasks significantly better when working with a partner in comparison to working alone. This is also true in the more game-like MMOGs (Steinkuehler, 2004).

Some of the more interesting findings from VW research have mentioned the idea that these environments give real world and hands on opportunities to learners—interesting findings indeed in a virtual environment that you can't touch! In some cases, VWs have been used to provide experiences for learners that are either impossible or impractical in RL. Roussou (2004) used a VW to allow students to encounter virtual environments such as the workshop of the Ancient Greek sculptor Phedias, where they could help him to create the statue of Zeus for Olympia. Bani et. al (2009) followed a similar path when they had their students learn by creating historical buildings such as the Tower of Pisa. In both of these cases, travel to the sites in question would have been too expensive (Pisa) or simply impossible (ancient Greece). Rather than recreating structures, a study by Gu, Gul, Williams and Nakapan (2009) created an architectural studio in SL where students created their own works that were then judged.

Not all such education work in SL connects to building and history. Antonacci and Modaress (2005) discussed the creation of a SL medical clinic where their medical students from the University of Kansas Medical Center could practice their patient care prior to working on real people. From the RL world of business, studies have found positive benefits both for issues related to marketing (Belei, Noteborn, & de Ruyter, 2009; Fassler, 2009) and purchase marketing (Jæger & Helghein, 2009).

Jarmon, Traphaga, Mayrath, and Trivendi (2009) summarize the potential advantages of using VWs for education in this way:

> (a) the capacity to host virtual social interactions and collaborations, (b) the capacity to allow users to test hypothesis by applying them to an actual project and doing something active (Kalyuga, 2007), without the risk and cost of the real world, (c) the possibilities for relevance of their virtual actions to the real world, (d) the capacity to allow for various types of activities to be practiced and demonstrated virtually, (e) the stimulation of imagination, exploration, and creativity, and (f) an increased sense of personal presence and tangible experience in the virtual world. (p. 179)

While some of the advantages they point out also apply to the wider area of CMC, it is clear that VWs have strengths—and no doubt weaknesses—that separate them from other forms of CMC. Some of these strengths will be discussed in the final chapters of this book.

Summary

This chapter began with an examination of some of the theories that help to explain why VWs have potential applications to language learning. Although many of these theories were created long before the creation of the first VW, the learning that takes place in virtual environments is still in many ways the same. The chapter then examined some of the existing research into both CMC and VWs, highlighting the findings that suggest potential applications of these technologies to language learning, as will be discussed in more detail in later chapters.

Suggested Readings

Print Resources

Dewey, J. (1939). *Experience and education.* New York: The Macmillan Company.

Molka-Danielsen, J. & Deutschmann, M. (eds.) (2009). *Learning and teaching in the virtual world of Second Life.* Trondheim: Tapir Academic Press.

Palfrey, J. & Gasser, U. (2008). *Born digital: Understanding the first generation of digital natives.* New York: Basic Books.

Winder, D. (2008). *Being virtual: who you really are online.* Chichester: Wiley.

Vygotsky, L. (1978). *Mind in society: The development of higher mental processes.* Cambridge: Harvard University Press.

Wankel, C. & Kingsley, J. (eds.) (2009). *Higher education in virtual worlds: Teaching and learning in Second Life.* Bingley, UK: Emerald.

Web-based Resources

Learning-Theories.com (2011). Retrieved October 22, 2011 from <http://www.learning-theories. com/>.

Learning Theory (education) (2011). Retrieved October 19, 2011 from Wikipedia: <http://en.wikipedia. org/wiki/Learning_theory_%28education%29>.

Chapter 4: Virtual Worlds, Spaces, and Faces

> And just as a daydreamer forgets his actual surroundings, and sees other realities, so Pollack drifted, detached, his subconscious interpreting the status of the West Coast communications and data services as a vague thicket for his conscious mind to inspect and interrogate for the safest path [...] (Vernor Vinge, Portal, 1986).

Introduction

As demonstrated in Chapter 2, there are a variety of Virtual Worlds currently available, many of them with strong potential for language learning. However, as discussed in the previous chapter, it is also clear that the vast majority of the research currently being conducted on this topic is taking place in Second Life. This is no doubt partly due to the wide array of educational, social, and collaborative environments available there, as will be discussed in Chapter 5 of this text, and also due to the large and diverse user base and large virtual landmass of that VW. Because of this popularity, this chapter will take examples from SL, starting with an examination of the languages currently represented in that VW, and continuing with an examination of the results of a survey which looked at language use and language learning in Second Life. The chapter concludes with a deeper discussion of the role of the avatar in VWs.

In Chapter 2 I discussed the difficulty of gathering concrete and reliable data relating to the user numbers for VWs. This is partially due to the policy of most VWs to never delete existing accounts, even if the user has only logged in once...years ago. This makes the use of overall user numbers problematic since the percentage of active users may be substantially lower than the total number of accounts. While the user total of Second Life is stated as being approximately 19 million, the number of those individuals who logged in within the last 60 days is actually closer to 1.5 million[8]. Although this is still an enormous number of participants, it is only 12.7% of that larger total. In addition, these numbers tell us nothing about how long these users are actually in-world—twelve minutes versus twelve hours both count as a single log. Fortunately, SL also makes available user statistics based on user hours for each business quarter.

The countries shown in Figure 4.1 represent those with the highest number of user hours for the third quarter of 2009 (July–Sept)[9]. These numbers are based on the total time avatars were logged into SL, so this would include time spent alone, shopping, or even doing nothing. This also includes possible times logged into SL by bots—a problem briefly discussed in Chapter 2. Nonetheless, these numbers can provide a much more accurate picture of which countries are currently active in this VW, and how much time those users are spending in the world. During the third quarter of 2009, there were a total of 118,071,244 user hours in SL. Of those approximately 118 million hours, 111.4 million are represented by the 28 countries shown in Figure 4.1 (93.8% of total user hours). The total number of user hours by country contains 250 entries, but this includes a number of territories (e.g. American Samoa) and regions (e.g., Antarctica).

8 Based on data from SL website on March 29th, 2010.
9 This data available at: <https://blogs.secondlife.com/community/features/blog/2009/11/02/the-second-life-economy--third-quarter-2009-in-detail>.

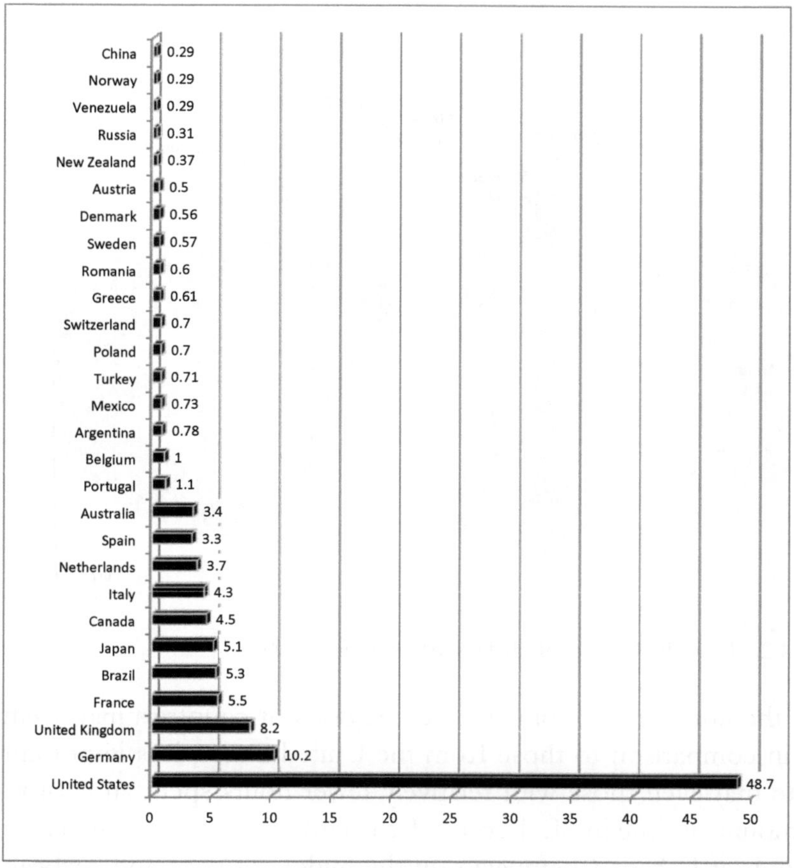

Figure 4.1: Top Countries in SL (user hours in millions, 3rd quarter 2009)

The countries with SL user hours range from Afghanistan to Zimbabwe and there are users hours representing every continent (see Figure 4.2). The 46% of the user hours seen in Figure 4.2 represented by North America include the United States, Canada, Mexico, Central America, and the Caribbean; so this potentially includes speakers of English, Spanish, French, and a wide variety of other languages since it is quite likely that a number of languages other than English were being utilized by users even within the United States.

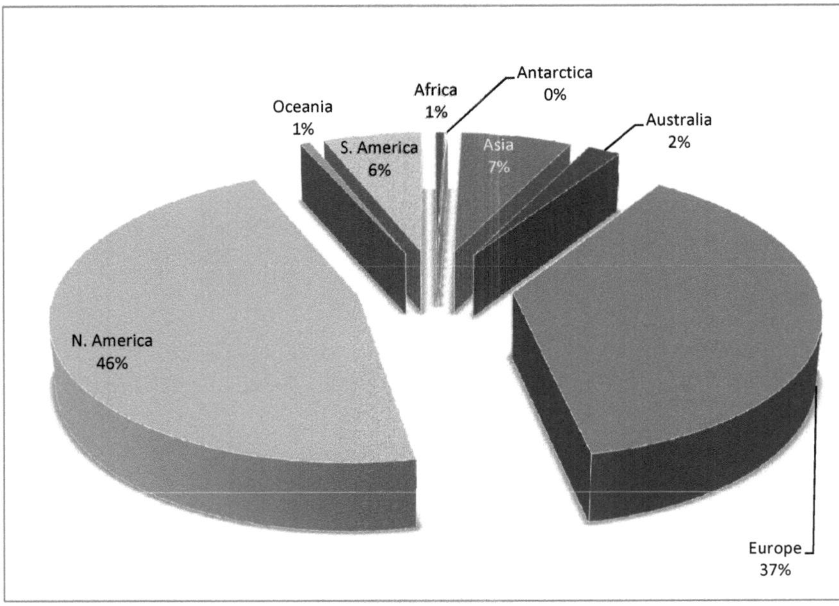

Figure 4.2: SL use by Continent (3rd Quarters hours, 2009)[10]

While the numbers for some of these regions or countries may seem small in comparison to those from the United States, it is important to note that even those with relatively fewer hours spent an enormous amount of time in SL. Because I currently teach at the University of Illinois at Urbana-Champaign (in the middle of corn and soybean fields two hours south of Chicago), access to some languages can be problematic. Therefore, the 570,000 users hours spent in-world by residents of Sweden (though only about 1.2% of the hours spent in-world by US members) provide opportunities for students at my university to practice that language that are simply not available here on our RL campus.

As can be seen above in Figure 4.1, a number of the countries listed share the same language (e.g., Mexico and Venezuela). Although Second Life does not provide statistics on the language (or

10 Continents and Oceania classified based on United Nations criteria. Antarctica percentage actually .04%, but reads as 0% due to rounding.

languages) spoken by each user a rough approximation of the most common languages is possible, as shown in Figure 4.3. The 112 million user hours represented by the speakers of these languages account for 94.9% of the total number of hours spent in Second Life by users world-wide.

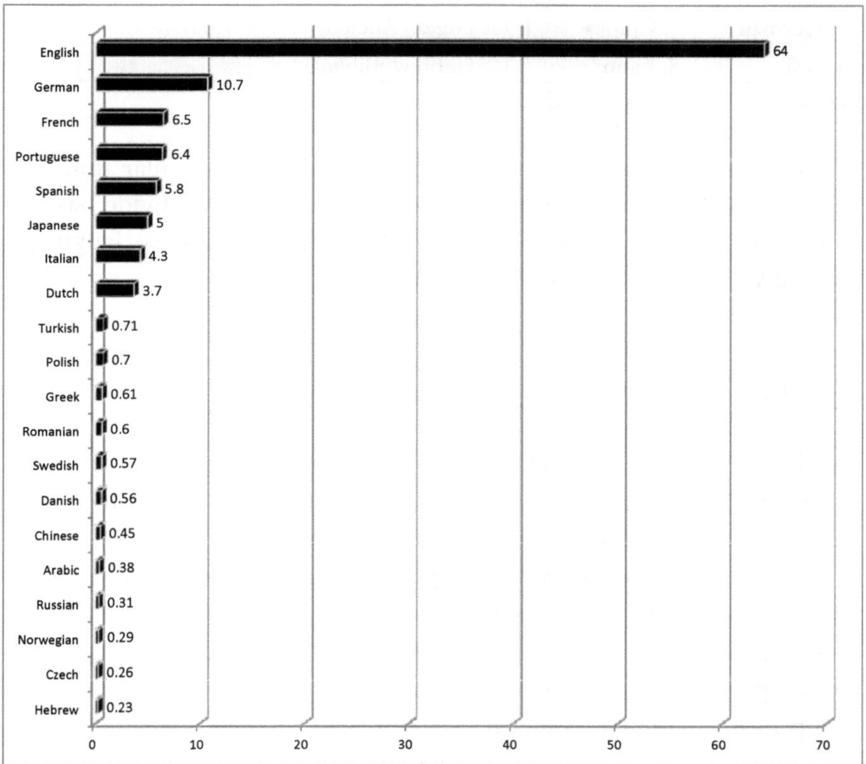

Figure 4.3: Top 20 Languages in Second Life (3rd Qtr. 2009, in millions of user hours)[11]

According to research by Furman, Goldberg, and Lusin (2007) the top languages studied in the United States at the higher education level range from Spanish to Korean (see Figure 4.4). All of these lan-

11 It is important to note that this figure is a rough approximation and does not take into account countries with multiple languages (e.g., in the case of Canada, only English is represented in the figure).

guages are represented in the top 20 most common languages in SL, with the exceptions of American Sign Language (ASL), Ancient Greek, Biblical Hebrew, and Korean.[12]

1. Spanish	5. Italian	9. Russian	13. Portuguese
2. French	6. Japanese	10. Arabic	14. Hebrew
3. German	7. Chinese	11. Greek, Ancient	15. Korean
4. ASL	8. Latin	12. Hebrew, Biblical	

Figure 4.4: Top languages studied in the United States in 2006

While no reliable research seems to exist providing similar numbers for the most popular languages being studied on a worldwide basis, it is safe to say that many of the most popular additional languages studied worldwide are also represented in Figure 4.4.

A Survey of SL Language Use, and Language Learning

As shown above, VWs like SL provide potential access to both a wide variety of speakers of other languages, and also access to potentially many thousands of hours of input from those speakers. However, this information—while important—does not actually give a picture of what languages are being used in VWs like SL, and how they are being used (hence the italicized potentials). For example, while speakers of German constitute the second largest language group in SL, with 10.7 million user hours in the 3rd quarter of 2009, this does not tell us how many of those speakers of German are actually using that language in SL or what other language(s) they may be using instead. In addition, these general statistics do not provide

12 Although Korean did not make the top languages list, Koreans had almost 209 thousand user hours in the 3rd quarter, 2009. It is exceedingly difficult to find true native speakers of either Ancient Greek or Biblical Hebrew! It would be feasible to study ASL in SL, but doing so would require the use of custom designed HUDs created for that purpose.

us with any details about how—if at all—users of SL are practicing additional languages in the VW.

In order to answer these questions, I visited a random sample of sims in SL, offering users the chance to take a survey. The survey was distributed via a URL distributing interface as seen in Figure 4.5. Since this interface could be attached to my avatar, it gave me the capability to offer the survey to users in any sim. This is a critical feature since it is not possible to leave objects such as the interface out on the ground in most sims. Instead, users I approached or who saw the survey offer could click on one of the language choices on the interface, which would then take them to an online survey and also give them a note providing a short explanation of the survey in the language selected. Since Bell, Castronova, and Wagner (2009) mentioned the issue of users attempting to take a paid survey multiple times for the money, I mentioned in the survey introduction that only one survey payment would be made per IP address. Although it certainly would have been possible for some clever users to get around this restriction, the patterns of responses to the survey questions did not seem to indicate that this was a problem.

The survey asked questions related to 4 main topic areas:

- Background and Nationality
- Language Background
- Language Use in Second Life
- Educational Experiences in SL

The survey was distributed over an 11 day period, for a total of approximately 46 hours during which I visited over 400 regions in Second Life, resulting in 237 completed surveys. Since I sampled regions at random, a number of the sims visited contained no active users. This was easily determined by opening the "mini-map" in the SL interface at each sim (this map shows that avatars are present in a sim by putting a green mark on the map—one for each avatar). Determining the response rate to the survey was not possible since the survey was given out in a public manner. While a number of avatars who I approached with information about the survey declined to take it, many other avatars who saw the interface took the survey without approaching me directly. This could have been accomplished either by clicking the interface directly or perhaps by being given the URL to the survey by a friend.

Figure 4.5: Survey Interface

Among the 237 responders, the average age was 27.6, with a range from 19 to 64.[13] The majority of the users reported being in their upper 20s to lower 30s. As seen in Figure 4.6, the gender breakdown

13 This survey relied on self-reported data. Since this was collected in a VW (as opposed to face-to-face) there is no way to know with absolute certainty the true RL age, gender, language, etc. of the users. However, the same might be said of any survey collected in a manner other than face-to-face.

is not quite so simple, in keeping with previous findings by Gronstedt (2007). In Gronstedt's study, it was found that approximately twenty percent of real life males used female avatars in SL. I asked the respondents what gender they most often used in SL, since my own observations suggested that many users of SL have used more than one gender, but that they usually stayed with one choice. As seen in the Figure, RL males made up 65% of those surveyed in comparison to 35% for women.

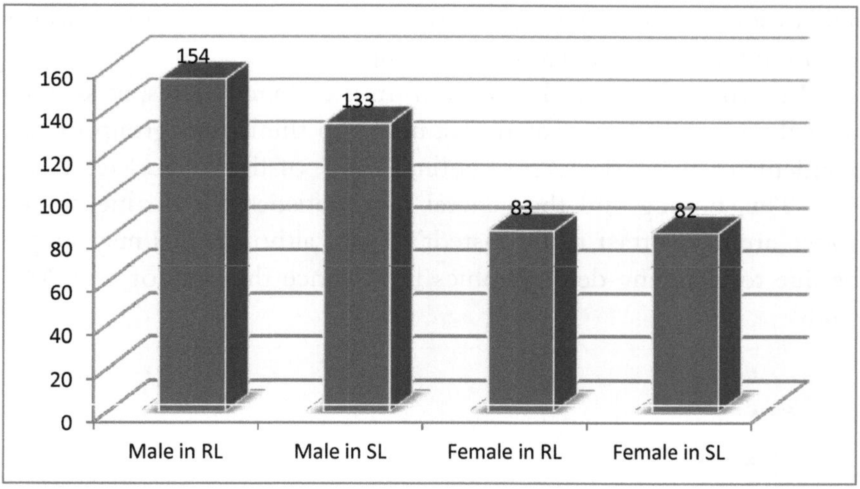

Figure 4.6: Gender Breakdown in SL (T=237)

However, when it comes to SL, 21 (13.6%) of the RL males said that they usually used a female avatar in SL. Only one RL female used primarily a male avatar in SL. This means that among those sampled, SL male avatars made up only 56% of the population surveyed. While this survey was not meant as a linguistic examination of the kinds of language used in SL (i.e. examining specific speech acts, etc.), this is clearly an area that is rich in research potential.

It is also worth noting that since the time of this survey, SL has greatly increased the number of default avatars that users may choose from when registering for their account. In the earliest versions of the environment, users were offered two choices—one male avatar and one female. At the time of the survey there were 8 offerings—4 for males and 4 for females. However, in mid-2011 Second Life greatly expanded their choices to 45 default avatars, with additional options available in the inventory library folder which can be accessed in-world. In addition to the 11 human avatars (6 female and 5 male) there are also animal, robot, and vehicle avatars to choose from. This means that it is no longer always clear from appearance whether a new avatar in Second Life is male or female. At a recent meeting on EduNation, I witnessed a new group of students which included several males and females but also 2 blimp avatars, a tank, and various robots. Once again, this creates a research and learning situation that is both dynamic and complex.

In terms of Nationality, users from the United States, in keeping with the overall SL user statistics, made up the largest group of respondents of the survey, representing 27.4% of the replies (see figure 4.7). This finding and the general user statistics for SL mentioned above are in contrast to Gronstedt's work, although this may simply be due to changing demographics in SL since the time of that 2007 study.

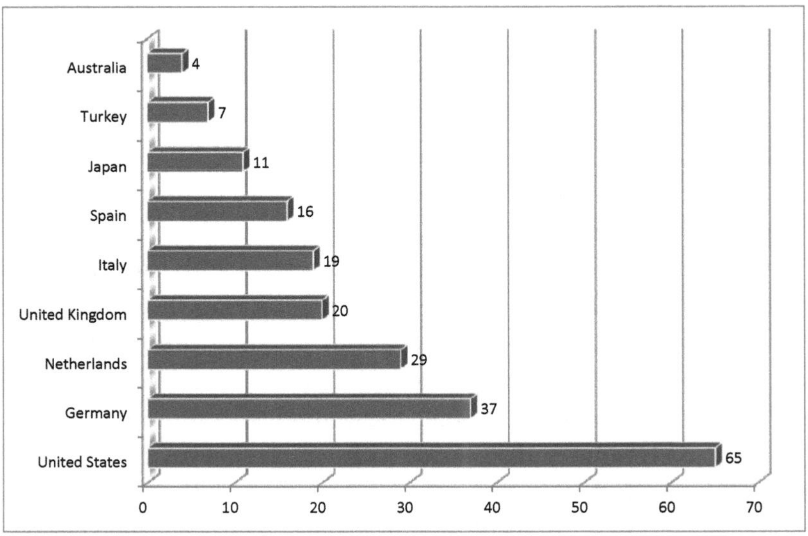

Figure 4.7: Top 10 Countries Responding to Survey

While the results of this survey in terms of country representation differ somewhat from the general demographics presented by SL, all the countries shown in Figure 4.7 are from the top 16 countries as reported by the SL data. Overall, there were representatives from 20 countries that responded to the survey, but three countries had only two respondents (France, Canada, and Portugal), and the remaining seven countries had only a single respondent (China, Egypt, Mexico, New Zealand, Romania, Sweden, and Venezuela). These ten countries are not represented in the Figure 4.7. In determining the users' language backgrounds, the survey asked what language they used most often in RL[14] (see Figure 4.8).

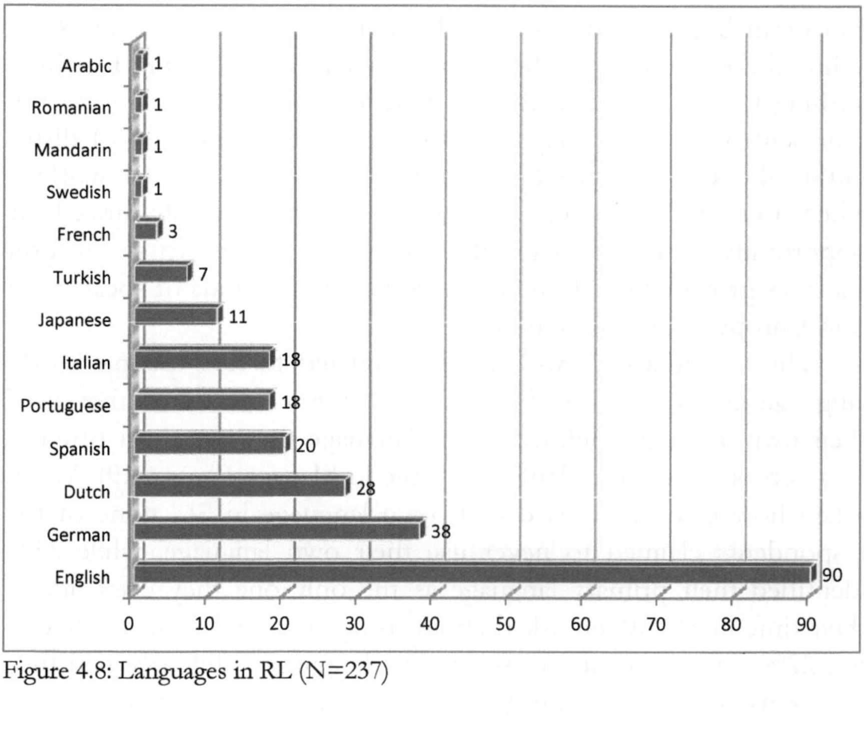

Figure 4.8: Languages in RL (N=237)

14 A more detailed analysis of language backgrounds in underway in an expanded version of this survey which will be submitted for publication in 2012.

As shown in the figure, speakers of English, representing the United States, the United Kingdom, Australia, and New Zealand, make up the largest percentage of the respondents (37.9%). Although there were actually 93 respondents from those 4 countries, 2 of the U.S. participants identified Spanish as their primary language and one of the Canadians was a speaker of French. However, one of the residents of the Netherlands was a native speaker of English, resulting in a total of 90 primary speakers of English. The only other unexpected result was a single Italian who identified German as her primary language. As shown, the vast majority of the participants in the survey came from European language backgrounds (this includes speakers of English, Spanish, and Portuguese who were not living in European countries), with only 20 of the respondents coming from a non-European background (Arabic, Mandarin, Japanese, and Turkish[15]). While these numbers might seem somewhat discouraging for those wishing to use a VW to learn or practice one of the languages not represented here, this may be partially due to the method of distributing the survey. Since I may have often been asleep or working when users from Asia were in-world, I may have simply missed the opportunity to ask them to take the survey. As shown in the user statistics provided by SL, there are certainly thousands of speakers of non-European languages in SL.

The survey asked two questions related to how people used[16] language in Second Life. First, it asked them how often they used their own language (defined as the language they use most often in RL) versus some other language while in SL (see Figure 4.9). When asked how often they used their own language in SL, none of the respondents claimed to never use their own language, while 31% identified their primary language as the only one they used during their time in SL. When asked about using another language while in SL, 22% claimed to never use another language, while 0% said they always used another language. At first glance, this finding does not

15 Though some might certainly argue that Turkish is a European language.

16 While it is most common to use "speak a language," a great deal of the communication in SL is accomplished via text chat.

seem in keeping with the responses pertaining to primary language use. After all, if 31% reported only using their primary language, then how could it be that only 22% claimed that they never used another language? Although the reason for this difference is not entirely clear, it may be due to the fact that these were separate questions on the survey, and on different pages of the online form. In addition, it may be that explicitly admitting to never using another language may have been seen as face-threatening. It is also possible that a person who was considering clicking on the "never use another language" choice remembered that they did speak a few works of Spanish to another avatar.

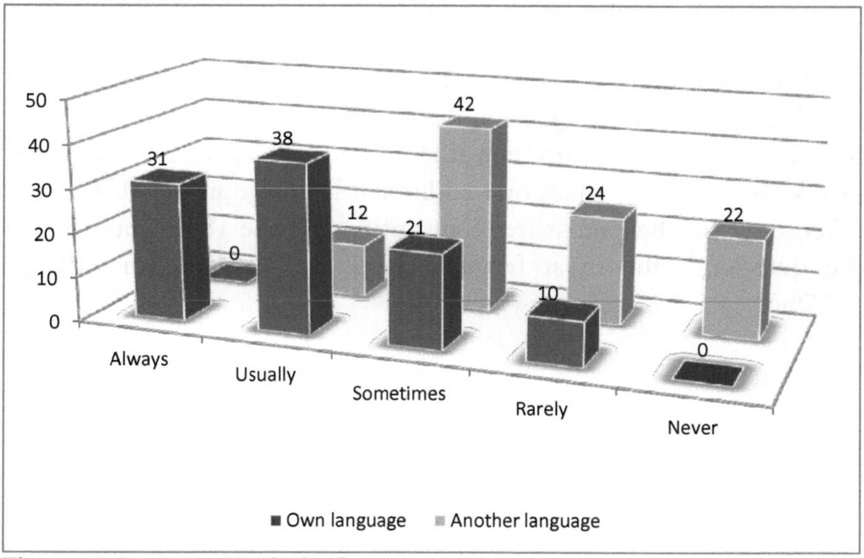

Figure 4.9: Language Use in SL (by percentage)

Whatever the reason for the discrepancy, 54% of the participants either usually or sometimes use another language while in SL, with 78% claiming that they communicate in another language in SL at some time. If this claim holds true, then it means that there is an enormous amount of second (or third, or fourth…) language practice occurring in VWs like SL on a daily basis.

Perhaps not surprisingly, the largest group that never spoke another language in SL was comprised of English speakers (25). Other individuals who never spoke another language were represented by Spanish (7), German (6), Japanese (5), Portuguese and Spanish (4 each), and Turkish (1). While some might maintain that speakers of English had a high number of individuals who never used another language in SL due to the lack of language learning in the U.S., there are certainly other explanations. First and foremost because native speakers of English are the largest group in SL, it is usually easy to find people speaking that language, and the need to speak another language is not a necessity. Second, as will be discussed below, many people who do speak a second language in SL chose English for their communication.

Following up on the question related to other language use, I also asked what other language(s) they most often made use of while in SL (see Figure 4.10). Although it is very likely that many of the respondents used more than one additional language in SL, this survey asked only for their most frequent option. Of the 185 responders to the question,[17] the most frequent response was English with 79 (42.7%).

17 185 respondents since the 52 (22%) individuals who said they never used another language automatically skipped this question.

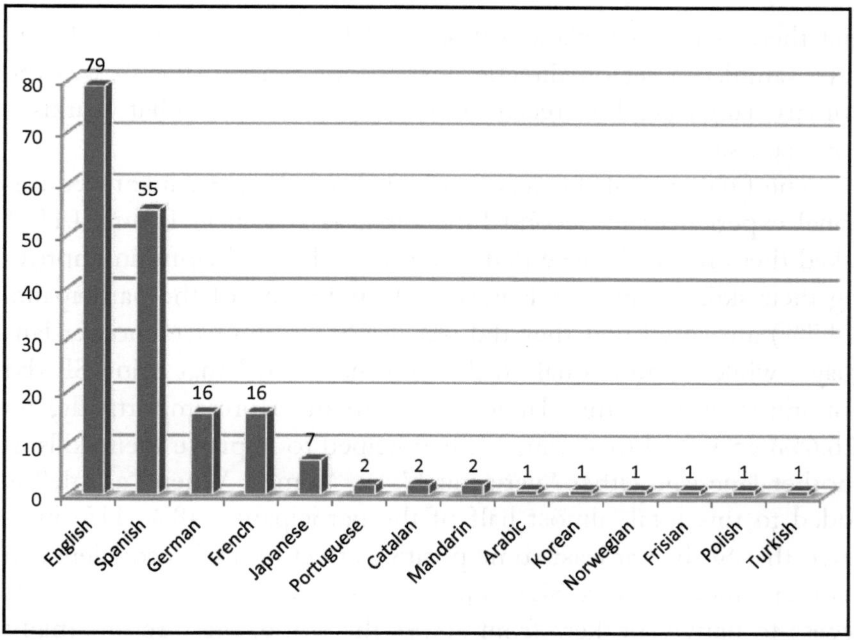

Figure 4.10: Other Languages used in SL (N=185)

In fact, English was the most frequently used other language amongst each language group identified in this survey. SL users who used Spanish as their most frequent other language were second, with 55 (29.7%). Of those selecting Spanish as the other language they most frequently use in SL, 47 were from the United States. Given that Spanish is overwhelmingly the most popular second language to study in that country, this result is not a surprise. Though the language statistics presented in these charts may give the impression that some languages (e.g., Polish and Korean in Figure 4.10) are little used in SL, it is important to note that this is an artifact of the survey itself.

As noted earlier, at other times of the day, some of these language numbers may have been higher. In addition, SL covers a truly massive virtual land area—millions of square kilometers—divided into many thousands of regions. Since I sampled these regions randomly, rather than attempting a stratified sample based on the language(s) used in the region (which would be simply impossible given that there is no such classification available), this means that I may have sampled a region directly next to one where Turkish was the primary language, but received no responses from that Turkish-dominant sim.

The final area of the survey asked about the participant's educational experiences in Second Life. First, as shown in Figure 4.11, I asked them if they believe that using SL had been helpful in improving their skills in another language. As noted, 35 of the participants (14.7%) answered that they did not use SL to improve another language, while an additional 16.5% (39) maintained that using SL did not improve any other language for them. More importantly, 63 (26.6%) answered that using SL had helped to improve their skills in another language either "very much" or "some." When "a little" is added to this total, almost half of the participants (48%, 115) indicated that SL had at least some positive effect on their proficiency in another language. Since SL can provide language learners with instant access to native speakers from across the world, these results might be expected. However, the question is to what extent SL really has improved the language skills of these respondents. Of course, there is no pre-post TOEFL data regarding the effect of SL on these users (though it would be a worthy study).

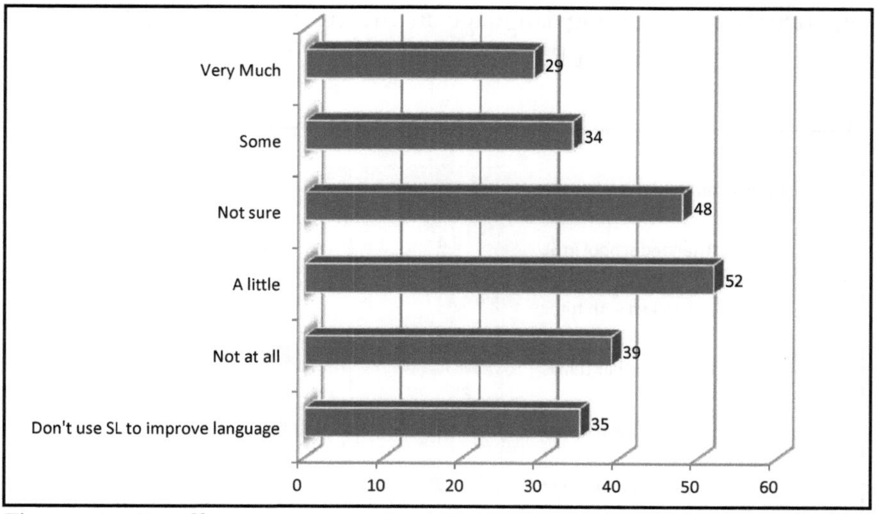

Figure 4.11: SL Effect on Language (N=237)

The final question to be addressed in the survey asked how the participants used SL to improve their additional language skills. As shown in Figure 4.12, this question provided nine possible responses and the participants (the 202 who said they use SL in an attempt to improve their other language(s)) were told to mark all answers that applied to them. For each possible answer, more detailed information was given in the actual survey (e.g. sample school names in SL, what "school" means for the purpose of the survey, etc.). As seen in the figure, the most popular method of improving their language skills was to listen to audio chat. While this may seem a strategy to improve listening skills, it must be noted that if a user's voice function is active in SL, then she will hear any voice chat around her—and at a greater distance than text chat is discernable—unless she "mutes" it. Therefore, the popularity of this response may be partially due to not being able to escape listening. The next most popular response, joining a group, did not specifically address groups meant for language practice. This might include any number of role play groups, interest groups, dance club groups, etc. where any one of the languages being used was one they were learning. Interestingly, the two least common practices for improving language in SL are the most traditional or formal ways to do so in RL.

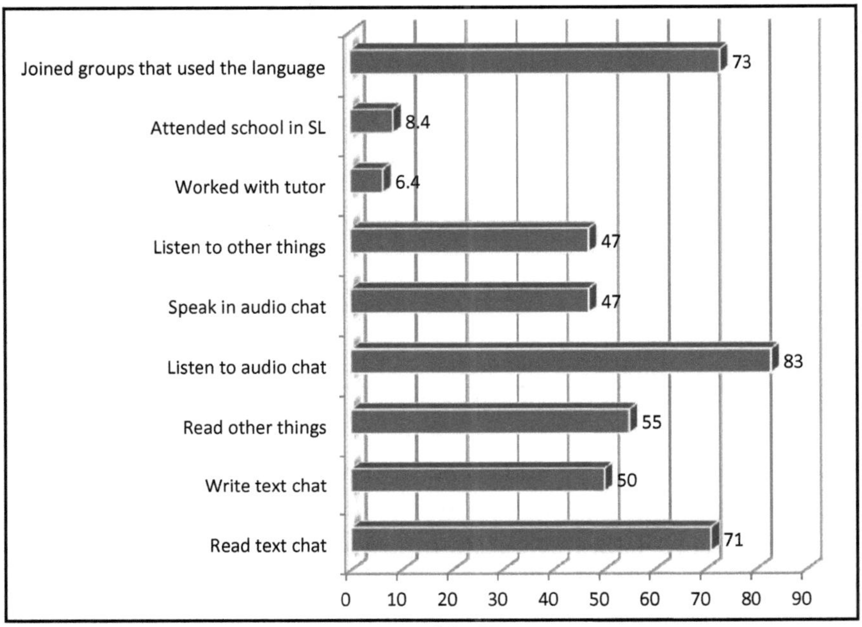

Figure 4.12: How Language was Improved in SL

While the theorists discussed in Chapter 3 would likely be unsurprised with this observation, there are other explanations for this as well. First, schools or tutoring in SL may cost money, and many users of SL have a distinct lack of Lindens (the currency used in Second Life) to spend on education. Second, it may be that going to school in SL, especially if it is a more formal virtual classroom, would remove the play component that most users initially came to SL looking for. In other words, it might change it from play to work.

Overall, as seen in this section, it is apparent that there is a great deal of language happening in SL. As illustrated in the data from SL— which again must be taken with a grain of salt—there are hundreds of millions of user hours in Second Life each year, by users from every continent, who cover a wide variety of language backgrounds. It is also clear, based on my own survey data, that SL is not only the site of linguistic diversity, but also of extensive language practice.

The Avatar

> When thinking about how social life gets created online and how its attendant communication occurs, avatars are particularly powerful artifacts to consider. They prove to be the material out of which relationships and interactions are embodied: much as in offline life with its corporeal bodies, digital bodies are used in a variety of ways—to greet, to play, to signal group affiliation, to convey opinions or feelings, and to create closeness. [...] Avatars form one of the central points at which users intersect with a technological object and embody themselves, making the virtual environment and the variety of phenomena it fosters real. (Taylor, 1999: 41)

As discussed in Chapter 2, and reiterated in the quotation above, the avatar is a key component in any VW, whether it is text-based (as in the earliest VW environments), contains simple cartoon-like graphics, or is the rich 3-D environment of a modern VW.

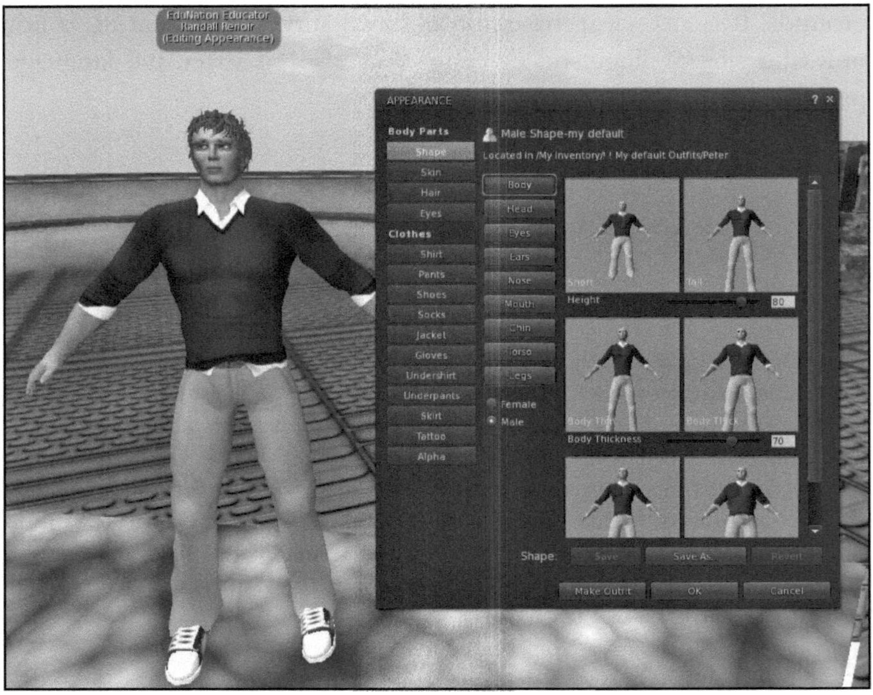

Figure 4.13: Modify Appearance Screen in SL

This section discusses how avatars are customized, move, and—most importantly—communicate in Second Life.

Appearance

Avatars can be customized in almost all VWs, and SL is no exception. While making an avatar more glamorous may seem inconsequential in the realm of language learning, there have been a number of studies that have examined the effect of avatar appearance both on the confidence of the owner of that avatar and how other avatars relate to that individual. (e.g., Taylor, 2002, Banakou, Chorianopoulos, & Anagnostou, 2009) or on how avatar eye gaze influenced communication patterns (Garau, Slater, Bee, & Sasse, 2001).

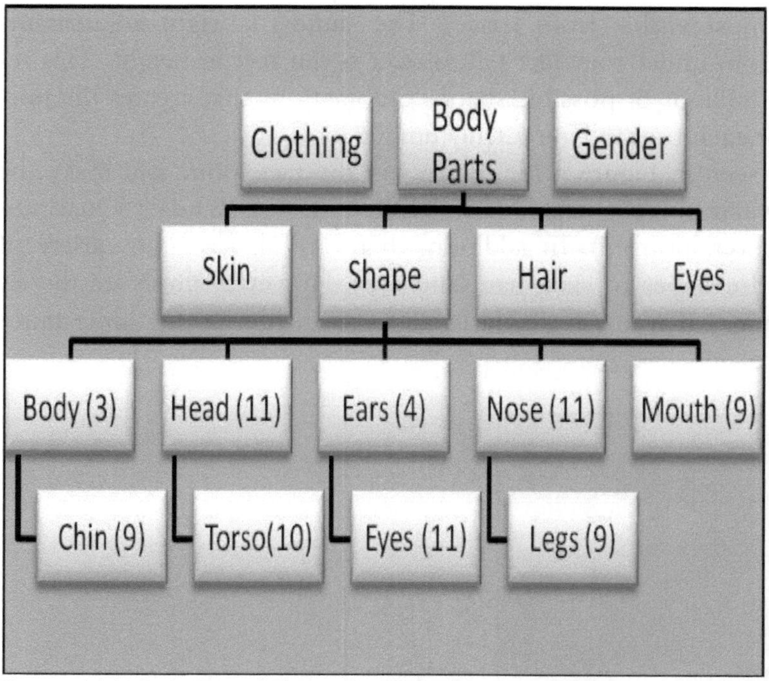

Figures 4.14: Overview of Shape Configurations

As seen in Figure 4.13, SL has a built-in interface for making some standard changes to avatars. This is accessed by right-clicking on an avatar (this only works on your own avatar, of course) and selecting "my appearance" from the pop-up list. As seen in the figure, appearance may be customized in 3 general categories: Body Parts, Clothes (both of these visible on the left-most column), and Gender (two radio buttons). Each of those categories has a number of subcategories (e.g. four under body parts), with additional sub-levels under those.

In the sub-category of shape alone (as seen in Figure 4.14), there are 9 subcategories, and under those are a total of 77 possible feature changes. For example, under ears may be found four settings: ear size, ear angle, attached earlobes, and ear tips. In addition, each one of these most specific features (e.g., earlobes) can be changed on a scale. Ear size can be set anywhere between zero (barely visible) to

100 (almost visible from space). The standard height adjustments range from under four feet tall to over seven feet in height. This results in millions of possible shape combinations that creates the possibly for each user to have a truly unique look.

As seen in Figure 4.15, changes in the face alone can make the same avatar unrecognizable (Randall Renoir, top; Randall "Quasimodo" Renoir, bottom). In addition, there are also a large variety of standard changes to skin, hair, and eyes. However, these are merely the changes that are available to all users in the modify appearance interface.

Figure 4.15: facial changes

In addition, many avatars are heavily modified with custom features. Because users are able to create items in Second Life (more on that below), there are many businesses in-world that sell items created to modify avatars beyond the standard changes. One change that helps to identify who is a noob versus an experienced user is the purchase of a skin. Skins are available that can give the appearance of any race, and also for races and species that go far beyond human. Many avatars also have hair that goes beyond the standard.

Other users are not content to stick with human-type avatars at all. As seen in Figure 4.16, there is also a thriving business in SL in creating avatars that cover almost any possibility.

Figure 4.16: Avatar Types

A recent search on Second Life Marketplace™ (an online shopping site for all things related to SL) for the term avatars resulted in possibilities including:

- Complete Human Female (2,736) and Male (1,273) Avatars
- Complete Fantasy and Sci-fi Avatars (4,859)
- Complete Robot Avatars (1,056)
- Complete Animal Avatars (1,549)
- Complete Anime Avatars (1,036)

The first category in this sampling of the results includes avatars ranging from elves, to Alice in Wonderland, to androids. Given the enormous number of standard changes that may be made to avatars, taken in conjunction with the changes which can go beyond standard, it is safe to say that each avatar in SL can be whatever he or she wishes to be.

As seen in Figure 4.16, in addition to the human avatars that make up the majority of SL users, three other common varieties include fantasy avatars, as seen in the hobbit on the right; animal avatars such as the Bengal tiger, and mechanical avatars. In addition, as mentioned earlier in this chapter, SL has also recently expanded on the number of default avatar types, adding animal, robot, and vehicle avatars choices for new members. While avatars which go beyond human types may not initially seem relevant to language learning, there are many thousands of sims in SL and other VWs dedicated to role play (RP) activities. While some of these RPs are almost certainly not appropriate for classroom use due to their adult nature, others are sites of large amounts of G-rated or PG-rated language practice (more on this in Chapter 5).

Movement and Interaction

Avatar movement in Second Life (and most other VWs), whether it be by land, air, or water, is accomplished either via the use of a computer keyboard or through a movement interface within SL. As seen in figure 4.17, the SL interface that controls movement has two primary features: direction of movement and type of movement. By left-clicking and holding down with a mouse on the movement arrows, the avatar on the screen will move in the indicated direction. In addition, the three buttons on the bottom of the interface may be clicked to control walking, running or flying (yes, avatars can fly).

Avatars can also move via the keyboard interface, typically through the use of the arrow keys, with the "page up" and "page down" buttons controlling flying. As with appearance, an issue as simple as movement may not seem worthy of discussion. However, as any user new to a VW like SL can tell you, the initial learning curve on something as simple as walking is a bit steep. Many of my own students who I've worked with in SL spend the first class session or two trying to figure out: 1) how they became stuck in a tree, wall, plant, etc., and 2) how to get out. However, after a few days of exploring, movement becomes natural and unconscious for most users.

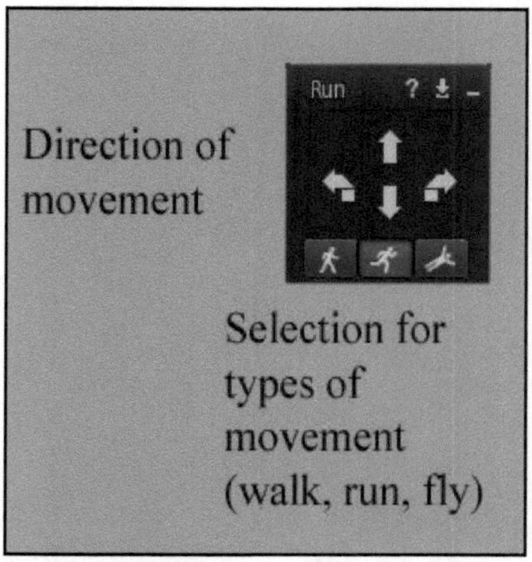

Figure 4.17: SL movement controls

Virtual Communication

In the old days of most VWs (say around 2007) avatars were often limited to text-based communication, but the majority of Virtual Worlds today have a wide variety of communication options that are of potential use for language learners.

Chat: Text and Voice

As illustrated in Figure 4.18, communication in VWs is not limited to human-to-human discussions.

Figure 4.18: Text-Based Communication

In this case, yours truly (in hobbit disguise complete with pipe weed) is using text-chat to communicate with a dragon (who assured me that she had already eaten her dinner) and a water fairy (shy, and therefore out of camera) in the medieval role-play sim, Avilion. In this communicative event, text was entered into the chat box on the lower-left side of the screen, which then appeared in a pop-up, as shown in the figure. Users may individually set how long such text will appear on their screens, a useful feature for both lower-level learners—who can have the text stay visible longer—and for more advanced learners—who may wish to have the text disappear sooner for enhanced reading practice.

In addition to the public chat that is shown in the figure, avatars also have the option to communicate in private chat which is only visible for the person it is sent to.

Text chat that has already disappeared from view may also be accessed via the chat log which appears when the small upwards-facing arrow is clicked next to the chat box. In addition, users can choose to have SL keep complete records of their text chat—public, private, or both—to be stored in a designated folder on their computer. This feature is particularly useful for language learners who wish to review a conversation or check on vocabulary they may have missed. Of course, it is also quite useful for nosey researchers (again, yours truly) who (after obtaining appropriate permissions) wish to keep complete records of communication.

In addition to text-based chat, many VWs—including SL—also integrate the ability to engage in synchronous oral communication with other avatars (see Figure 4.19). If voice chat is active a small white dot will remain above that avatar's head. This means that he is able to hear what other users are saying in open voice chat. As seen in the figure, if an avatar is speaking, the white dot turns into a green audio level indicator (though the green color does not show too well in this grayscale image).

Figure 4.19: Voice Chat

Users have the ability to individually adjust the incoming volume of other speakers by clicking on the voice control panel—accessed by clicking on the small upwards white arrow next to the speak button. This panel also gives users the ability to mute any active speaker so that they do not hear any of the voice chat from that user. As with text-chat, there is an option for private voice chat and also private group voice chat. The latter option is particularly useful for educational users as private chat (both text and voice) are distance-independent. This means that a teacher who is working with groups of students could have them based in distant areas of SL on team projects but remain in synchronous text and/or voice communication with all of them.

Nonverbal Communication

All VWs have the ability to use at least some forms of non-verbal (and non-standard-written communication). At its most basic, every VW has the ability to communicate with emoticons such as the smiley face :-) or a graphically-enhanced emoticon ☹. However, many VWs like SL also have included ways to communicate non-verbally that go beyond this. In SL, the gestures interface may be accessed by clicking on the gesture button, as seen at the bottom of Figure 4.20. The avatar in this image is demonstrating her feelings about my camera work with a shrug. As the figure shows, there are a variety of gestures available, ranging from dancing, to whistling, to the shrug shown. The can also be activated directly via text-chat using the shortcuts provided. More advanced users also may make use of HUDs (Heads Up Displays) which have been created for both gestures and specific facial expressions. Instead of bringing up the SL interface these are accessed by simply clicking a button on the screen to play the desired action.

For language learners and educators, this ability to engage in nonverbal communication is an important tool since one of the drawbacks of any form of distance communication (whether it be email, phone, or VW interaction) is that we lose the non-verbal feedback that we take for granted in RL. Just as an instructor's smile or nod in RL when listening to a student pronounce a new word correctly provides confirmation and encouragement to that student, an avatar smile or nod in a VW can have the same effect.

Figure 4.20: Gestures Interface

In addition to the default gesture animations that are available via the interface seen in figure 4.20, there are also hundreds of gestures available for free in SL, and many more (some of them quite elaborate) for sale either in-world or on the SL Marketplace This makes it easy for educators to create boxes of gestures for their students that include gestures and facial expressions that they will find useful in their own interactions, ranging from ones that raise a hand to ask a question to those indicating interest, boredom, or laughter.

Virtual Building

In a 2007 interview with the New York Times, Philip Rosedale (the creator of Second Life) mentioned that SL now contained over 1 billion in-world [user-created] "objects" occupying a total storage space of about 100 terabytes" (Dubner, 2007). While not all VWs allow users to create their own items in-world, many do so.

Figure 4.21: Building in SL

In the case of SL, to a greater extent than many other VWs, the vast majority of the content seen in the world, ranging from houses, to cars, to custom avatars, clothing, trees, and furniture, has been created by individual users of SL rather than the company that runs this VW.

All users of SL have access to the builder's interface shown in Figure 4.21. The interface provides detailed information about the highlighted pillar that has been selected for editing by the builder. In the objects tab visible in the picture, information is given that describes the exact position of the item in the sim via the X,Y,Z coordinates relative to the center of the sim. The panel also gives the size of the object being edited and its rotation in relation to its original position.

Most objects in SL are created using the basic units that are available via the builder's interface seen in Figure 4.22—the prim. As seen in the image, there are 15 basic prim shapes available, but these may be modified into many different sizes (from tiny to up to 64 square meters), linked together to form more complex objects, and the individual prims may also be given a number of different looks by using colors (free via the interface) and textures (many available for free and many thousands for sale) available in SL. The relatively small Greek Temple visible in Figure 4.21 was created using this interface and consists of 155 prims that have been shaped and linked together, and then modified with a number of different textures.

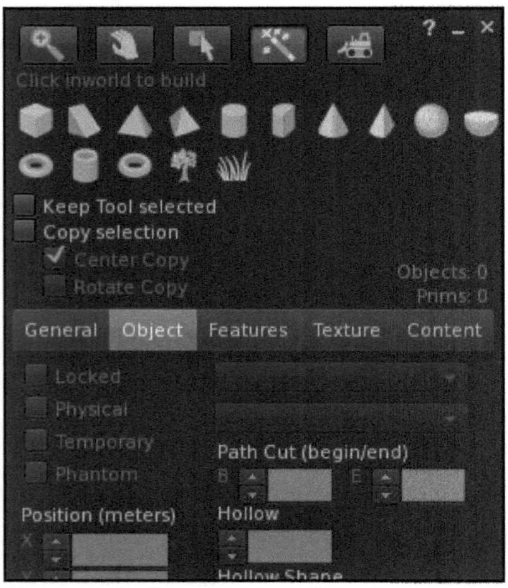

Figure 4.22: SL prims panel

While this chapter does not provide a complete guide to building in SL, I list several texts and websites at the end of the chapter that give detailed instructions and tutorials on the topic. For educators, the primary advantage of this ability to build things in a VW is that your possibilities are limited only by your imagination (and perhaps by limits on your time and bank account, but let us leave those issues aside for now). As will be discussed in the next chapter, there are already a large number of existing educational environments in SL that have been created by educators who are users of this VW. In addition, many builds with potential for educational use are available either at freebie locations around SL or for sale in-world or via Second Life Marketplace™.

Implications for Language Learning and Telecollaboration

Telecollaboration may take place using a wide variety of CMC tools, as discussed in Chapter 2 of this book. Indeed, this text also provides a number of examples of successful telecollaboration using tools such as email. However, as demonstrated in this chapter, Virtual Worlds, including Second Life, take the potential for telecollaboration into new areas due to the graphically-oriented 3D nature of these environments. Rather than collaborating with a partner at a distance who remains relatively faceless and voiceless (as in the case of email), VWs provide partners with an avatar of their choosing and an environment that encourages text-based, oral and non-verbal communication.

Virtual Worlds give us the ability to take our students out of the traditional classrooms criticized by Dewey (1939). We can use VWs (discussed further in Chapter 5) to create Dewey's more progressive schools where the students are active in their collaboration and where their interactions result in consequences, either positive or negative (Dewey, 1916). Virtual spaces also can provide educators and their students with opportunities to engage in "problem solving under adult guidance or in collaboration with more capable peers" (Vygotsky, 1978: 86) in a way that is simply not available with other forms of distance communication since VWs give us the ability to not only read and hear what fellow learners are communicating but see what they are doing and to collaborate in ways that were previously only possible in true face-to-face interaction in the physical world.

Summary

This chapter began with an examination of the user data available from Second Life for the third quarter of 2009. These numbers demonstrated both the large number of hours being spend in-world by users from around the world, and also the linguistic diversity in SL. Based on my own survey of users of SL, this chapter also examined exactly who is using SL, what the language backgrounds of those users are, and what type of language they are actually using within this world. Finally, we dug deeper into the world of SL, learning more about the avatar, in-world movement and communication, and building in SL.

Suggested Readings

Print Resources

Robbins, S. & Bell, M. (2008). *Second Life for dummies.* Indianapolis: Wiley.

Schroeder, R. (2002). *The social life of avatars: Presence and interaction in shared virtual environments.* London: Springer.

Weber, A., Rufer-Bach, K. & Platel, R. (2007). *Creating your world: The official guide to advanced content creation for Second Life.* Indianapolis: Wiley.

Web-based Resources

Curtis, A. (2011). How to build in Second Life. Retrieved September 22, 2011 from <http://www.uncp. edu/home/acurtis/New Media/SecondLife/HowToBuildInSecondLife.html>.

Official Second Life Video Tutorials on topics ranging from avatar appearance to building. Retrieved November 21, 2011 from <http://wiki.secondlife.com/wiki/Video_Tutorials#Official_Video_Tutorials>.

Saporito, J. (2011). The unofficial killer guide to building in Second Life. Retrieved December 4, 2011 from <http://www.killerguides.com/guide/second-life/ building>.

Virtual Worlds for Language Learning Wiki created for an 8-hour workshop teaching language teachers how to use SL. Retrieved December 1, 2011 from <http://sl4calico.pbworks.com/>.

Chapter 5: Language Learning in Second Life

> Have you ever had a dream, Neo, that you were so sure was real? What if you were unable to wake from that dream? How would you know the difference between the dream world and the real world? (Morpheus, The Matrix, 1999)

> There's actually a vibrant community of educators already in Second Life, and we're happy to see it continuing to grow. We've seen a range of academic and educational uses of the platform, from research to modeling to distance learning to real-time collaboration [...]. (Philip Rosedale, founder of Second Life, as interviewed by Dubner, 2007)

Introduction

Almost any setting in a Virtual World has the potential for language learning and telecollaboration. Just as in the real world, the key to the usability of any environment is the quality of the pedagogy that takes place there; even the best-equipped educational environment (whether in RL or a VW) is limited in its pedagogical potential if the teacher using that setting does not put adequate thought and effort into a sound pedagogical plan. While not all settings are appropriate for all learners, and while some settings would most certainly not work well for some classes, any location in a VW where the language under study is produced—written or oral—may benefit the learner. The trick, of course, is to determine what setting works for the purpose you wish to accomplish. As mentioned in the previous chapter, working with students in VWs can be challenging due to differences in the way communication, movement, etc. takes place in a VW in comparison to the Real World. However, it is important to note that what is "real" for our students may be quite different than the reality many of us grew up with:

> This idea [...] that cyberspace is becoming [...] our 'here', and that which isn't connected to cyberspace is becoming our 'there'. And when I [...] wrote Neuromancer, [...] the non-digital was our 'here' and the digital was our 'there'." (Gibson, 2007)

For many of our students—as argued by Gibson above—cyberspace (the Internet in all its forms) is just as real (here) for them as the non-digital used to be. They have matured in a world where books are no longer read on paper and where they never buy CDs, but go straight to digital copies that they bought (hopefully) online in the digital domain. They communicate with their friends via email, Skype video calls, blogs, or Twitter™. Communication via cyberspace is now "here" for them, and a transition to an increasing reliance on cyberspace—and VWs—for education is a logical continuation of this idea.

This chapter will provide an overview of educational environments in SL ranging from those connected to RL schools to ones that appear—at first glance—to not be connected to education at all. After providing an overview of VWs, the theory and research connected to them, an examination of how language is being used in Second Life and what types of educational environments exist there, there is one remaining question. How, exactly, can you teach language in a VW? This second half of this chapter will address this issue by looking at three methods for teaching language and culture in a VW: Telecollaboration, Simulations, and Tasks[18].

18 Prior to using any of these activities, it is expected that students are already familiar with the basic workings of SL. As mentioned previously, simple tasks like walking and communicating take time to master.

Language Learning and Telecollaboration Settings in SL

As mentioned above, it is the role of the educator to decide exactly how she wishes to use an educational space. While some RL classrooms are primarily spaces for the students to occupy while the professor lectures, other classrooms are much more dynamic spaces where the students interact with one other, their instructor, and visitors as part of the educational process. Indeed, the students may actually spend little time in these traditional classrooms, instead going outside the school to collaborate with fellow language learners or to engage with their local community if it includes members who speak the language they wish to learn. In this section three types of VW settings will be introduced: real-life schools that also exist in Second Life, schools which exist solely in the VW, and non-traditional educational settings in SL. While any of these settings may be used in the more traditional way (e.g. for virtual lectures), they may also be used as dynamic telecollaborative spaces where students can work with individuals or groups in virtual face-to-face or hands-on telecollaborative activities as described later in this chapter.

Real-Life Schools in Second Life

A recent query by the author via the SL search function for places that use the term university as part of their name resulted in over 450 hits. These included schools ranging from Arizona State University in the U.S. to a sim run by Waseda University in Japan. A search for college added an additional 120 results that appeared to represent RL colleges. However, these searches missed any colleges or universities that may have been listed in a language other than English. Given these numbers, it is safe to say that colleges and universities have a significant presence in SL. In many cases, as seen at the sim for Northern Illinois University (Figure 5.1), a prominent building or buildings from the RL campus is recreated in the SL setting. These buildings are frequently used for promotional purposes for the schools in question—typically containing information about the RL campus—but they also often have a number of meeting rooms for use by members of that school.

Figure 5.1: Glidden Campus: NIU (Northern Illinois University)

As was historically the case with MOOs (see Chapter 2), some faculty members and TAs use the virtual campus of their school for office hours or as collaboration sites. Unfortunately, many university sites are often empty unless there are faculty members at the school who are enthusiastic about the potential for VWs in their teaching. However, for educators working at schools with their own SL sites, many of these campuses have space on the sim that faculty members can use for their own projects, and most of these sims also have sandboxes—places where anyone can practice building things, or put out items they own. In conjunction, these latter features offer teachers at those schools with a site where they can design their own collaborative activities, as will be described later in this chapter.

It is difficult to get a true estimate of the number of schools[19] that exist either solely or mainly in Second Life since these institutions range from the very large to those run by individual teachers. Nonetheless, it is fair to say that these schools number in the thousands. One of the best-known schools that does not have a "brick and mortar" campus in the real world is Languagelab, which was founded in 2005.

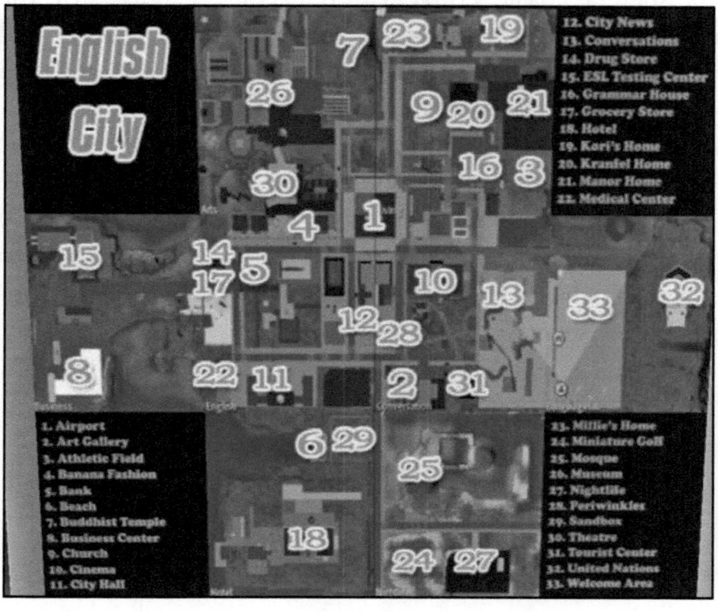

Figure 5.2: English City Map

This school is currently comprised of 20 interconnected islands (over 1.3 million square meters of virtual land) and was created to make use of the possibilities of SL for simulations (more on simulations

19 Many educators resist the label of "school" for the institutions they have created in Second Life because they do wish to escape the mindset of the traditional RL school environment. I use "school" in this chapter in the broadest sense.

later) to teach English as a Second Language. They currently offer more than 50 different classes and have students from over 50 countries. The Languagelab campus is build around English City (see Figure 5.2). As seen on the map, English City contains a wide variety of social and educational settings where the Languagelab teachers run classes. Although there are a large number of RL schools that are represented in SL, Languagelab is perhaps the most active school related to language learning in this VW. The courses at Languagelab include a number that might also be found in more traditional RL environments such as basic conversation classes, English for the TOEFL exam, and pronunciation courses, but these courses and others like Business English and English for Travel make use of a large variety of virtual setting available on their islands.

One of the more recent additions to the courses available at this school is English for Aviation. This course is in response to a change in the rules for the International Civil Aviation Organization (ICAO) which recently endorsed English language testing "in response to fatal accidents in which the lack of proficiency in English was identified as a contributing factor" (ICAO, 2011).

Figure 5:3: English City International Airport

As the majority of States around the world are ICAO members, it means that this recommendation affects many thousands of air traffic controllers. There are currently over 400 students working on this topic at Languagelab, with approximately 2,500 expected by the end of 2011.

These new courses take place at the English City International Airport (see Figure 5.3), which includes a large airport terminal, runways, service buildings, a control tower, and a number of planes and helicopters. Students in these courses work together, and with their instructor to replicate RL conditions as closely as possible. As seen in Figure 5.4, this means that the control tower interior includes stations for the air traffic controllers to work at as part of the English learning process.

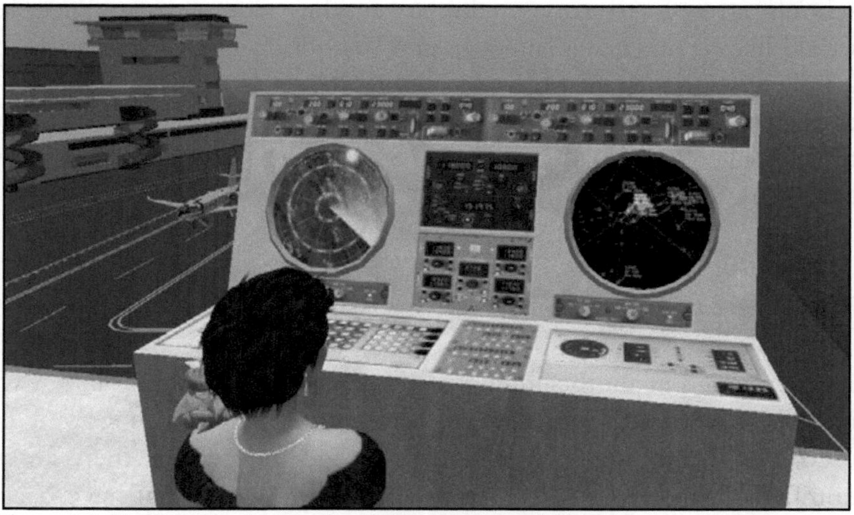

Figure 5.4: English City International Airport Control Tower

The instruction includes more traditional learning of English that relates to this job, but also engaging in virtual telecollaboration as they work side-by-side with other air traffic controllers who, in RL, may be located anywhere in the world. In this case, the school makes use of a number of original recording of communication between air traffic controllers who have a wide variety of accents and levels of

English proficiency (rather than the "perfect" communication normally used in most language classroom) in an attempt to replicate the often strained and unclear emergency situations that may occur for these individual in their RL jobs.

While many of the SL schools that focus on language learning have English as their focus (no doubt due to the number of people using SL to improve their English) there are a number of smaller (and some large) schools that are teaching other languages as well. Some sims, such as The Goethe-Institut, offer language courses as one of multiple services they offer. In this case, the institute in question is a SL-based cultural institute for Germany that also offers free German language courses as well as chat sessions, art exhibits, and a variety of other activities. Although some of these smaller language schools struggle to survive due to funding issues—many people would like to practice a language in VWs but do not wish to pay for it—there is a constant presence of these types of schools that is encouraging for the future of language education in SL. In addition to these smaller schools, there are also many individuals who do private language tutoring in SL.

Non-Traditional Educational Settings

As mentioned at the beginning of this chapter, any setting in a VW may have potential for language learning, depending on how it is used. For those interested in both language and culture, there are a number of famous locations from around the world that have been recreated—sometimes in amazing detail—in the virtual world.

Figure 5.5: Virtual Mont Saint Michel

Mont Saint Michel (Figure 5.5) is a virtual version of its RL namesake in Normandy, complete with hordes of tour buses parked down by the water, and a flooded causeway leading to the mainland. Although there is no guarantee of encountering French speakers here, the same might be said of the same location in RL. Other virtual recreations include the Eiffel Tower (several versions of that), New York City and the Statue of Liberty, the Chichen Itza archeological site (created by the Mexican tourism board), La Sagrada Familia Cathedral from Barcelona, Himeji Castle in Japan, and almost any other major cultural landmark or historical site that can be imagined. For lovers of culture who do not have the opportunity to travel to such location in RL, these virtual versions may give them some of that experience.

As indicated by the survey discussed in Chapter 4, the majority of the respondents who used SL to improve their language abilities did not do so in a school or tutoring setting. Indeed, most individuals practice their language skills in one of the thousands of social settings in SL. One of the most popular social environments in RL and SL are dance clubs, and some of the most active of these virtual clubs specialize in ballroom dancing, as seen in Figure 5.6.

Figure 5.6: Sweethearts Jazz Club

Because dancing in SL is easy—doing so only requires clicking on a dance ball—dancers are free to concentrate on communication with their dance partner instead. All of these SL environments (just as with RL environments) must be considered blank slates when it comes to education. All of these environments have potential for virtual collaboration.

Pedagogical Practice in VWs

VW collaboration and Intercultural Competence

As briefly mentioned in Chapter 2, telecollaboration is the use of any number of CMC tools for the purpose of collaboration, language exchange, and/or cultural exchange between two or more groups (see O'Dowd, 2006 for a detailed discussion of this topic). The goal of this sort of exchange is not necessarily to enhance the grammatical knowledge of the participants (although that certainly may happen), but instead to enhance the ability of an individual "[…] to interact effectively with people from cultures that we recognize as being different from our own" (Guilherme, 2000: 297). The end goal is to create speakers who are competent in intercultural communication. This sometimes may mean that what you say may not be as important as how you say it. As example of this issue comes from a study Hanna and Nooy (2003) conducted which examined their students' attempts to engage in communication on the discussion boards of the French newspaper Le Monde. They found that two students who had little success in engaging in discussion on the boards also happened to be among their more advanced pupils. At the same time, two students who were not linguistically advanced in French—and who even engaged in parts of their discussion in English—had much greater success due to their use of more culturally appropriate interaction on the forum. O'Dowd (2003) came to a similar conclusion in his study of an intercultural exchange between students studying Spanish and English, finding that students who believe their partners were interested in their own culture were likely to "write more and, possibly, to learn more themselves and change their attitudes towards the target culture" (p. 130). As might be imagined, the opposite also held true, with individuals who detected a lack of interest by their partner losing motivation.

According to O'Dowd (2006), there are five key components related to intercultural learning:

- Language learning cannot be separated from culture learning as language manifests many of the social actions of a society and expresses the values and beliefs which underlie these actions.
- Although cultures continue, to a great extent, to be equated with nations, increased importance is attributed to variation within cultures and the fact that each individual has a number of 'cultures' and identities.
- By culture learning, the social studies' sense of culture "[…] the attitudes and beliefs, ways of thinking, behaving and remembering shared by members of that community" (Kramsch 1996: 2) is seen as more appropriate than the humanities' tradition of focusing on history, literature and social institutions. These aspects are also seen as relevant, however it is their meaning and significance in the target culture and not the products and practices themselves which are attributed importance.
- The central aims of intercultural learning are seen as being able to interact successfully and establish relationships with members of the other culture(s) and to understand (in as much as this is possible) how members of other cultures see and interpret the world. Intercultural learning is therefore understood to be an interactive process which involves the development of skills, attitudes, cultural awareness as well as knowledge.
- As a result of learning about another culture, learners are expected to take a more critical and distanced view on their own culture and to come to an understanding that there can be no one universal way of understanding or interpreting cultural behaviour. (pp. 45–46)

The idea of cultural exchange is certainly not a new concept, having expanded rapidly—especially in Europe—after the Second World War, but the use of CMC tools in that process is a more recent innovation. This more recent telecollaboration had made use of tools such as email (e.g., Ballou, 2002; Ducate, 2003; O'Dowd, 2006; Murray and Bollinger, 2001), MOOs (Backer, 1999), forums (e.g., Hanna and Nooy, 2003; Wang, 1997), and videoconferencing (Ballou, 2002;

O'Dowd, 2000; Wang, 2004). These tools have given teachers and language learners a tremendous advantage in that cultural exchanges are now possible without either the expense of taking a class abroad for such an exchange or the long wait in a traditional snail mail pen pal exchange. While this is not such a problem in situations such as exchanges within Europe, exchanges between locations such as the United States and Japan are much more problematic.

Figure 5.7: Collaborative Space in SL

VW collaboration in Teacher Education

Telecollaboration has been shown to have definite benefits for increasing intercultural communicative competence, but CMC telecollaborative techniques have two primary disadvantages (with the exception of videoconferencing). First, unless pictures are exchanged, the classes or partners in CMC exchanges do not get to see or hear their partners. Second, with the exception of writing, these other forms of CMC are limited in their ability to provide opportunities for true hands-on collaboration. In this section I will describe several advantages for VW collaboration in intercultural exchanges.

While email exchanges and message board discussions are valuable components in enhancing intercultural communication, these technologies are somewhat limited in terms of their potential for both interaction and creativity. As an example of how a collaborative space can work in a VW, I will first describe a recent collaboration between students at the University of Illinois at Urbana-Champaign (UIUC) and at the Universitat Autonoma de Barcelona (UAB)[20]. My research partner (from UAB) and I constructed a virtual meeting place for the students within Second Life (see Figure 5.7).

Figure 5.8: 3Holodeck Environments

This space, shown in more detail below, provided the students with 50 square meters of virtual space in the sky 3,500 meters above EduNation. The space was used for group meetings, small group

20 An upcoming article will describe this project in greater detail.

discussions, student experiments in SL, and for work on joint projects related to the use of technology and language instruction. The small round disc seen in the center of the space is a holodeck interface that gave the students access to over 100 separate scenes that they could use for meetings, entertainment/play, or collaboration as needed. As shown in Figure 5.8, these scenes ranged from a treehouse, to a pyramid, to an office. In some of these scenes, such as the treehouse, freebies were hidden for the students to find.

These freebies usually had nothing to do with collaboration or language learning per se, consisting of items like scooters, dancing cows, bicycles, or other fun or potentially useful SL objects. At the same time, all of the items provided as freebies were carefully selected to encourage interaction amongst the participants—even if that interaction meant riding a scooter around the island together. These freebies were meant to be used as tools to build group cohesion and to provide opportunities for play for the group. In the case of the treehouse freebies, these objects were hidden in acorns that—if clicked—asked the user a question, with a correct response resulting in getting the item(s) in the acorn. While my acorn questions had to do with movie trivia, it would also be possible to ask questions about exchange partners' cities, cultures, etc. As might be imagined, one of the challenges in engaging in any telecollaboration that takes place at a great distance (or a 7-hour time difference) is finding a time to meet. Because of this difficulty, we arranged only three whole group meetings over the course of the collaboration, with the remaining meetings done in groups.

Figure 5.9: Scavenger Hunt

For our initial meeting, we arranged a scavenger hunt (Figure 5.9) that had the participants find items around EduNation, but that also required them to ask questions about their group members (who they would later work with on a group project described below). In addition to the central meeting area and holodeck, we also set up a number of small group meeting spaces in the sky both above and below the main area. All of these areas could be accessed via teleporters (very Star Trek) at the main area and had seating for up to ten avatars. Each small seating area was far away from the others to be out of sight and out of text and voice-chat range so that the groups could talk without distraction (see Figure 5.10). In this case, the students, being observed by Melinda Aristocrat (my SL collaborator—Melinda Dooly in RL) and I, are brainstorming ideas for a podcasting project each group will work on together.

Figure 5.10: Small Group Meeting Area.

The figure shows 3 students, one from Spain, while the other two attend school in the U.S. As future teachers, the students in this collaboration worked on podcasts that would be appropriate for elementary school students since the collaborators from Spain were beginning their student teaching and would use the podcasts with their students in Barcelona.

After brainstorming their ideas, the participants were then asked to produce a slideshow for SL, as seen in Figure 5.11. In order to produce the slideshow, the students created PowerPoint presentations in the real world, imported the images into SL, and placed those slides into the slide presenters shown in the image (also seen from a distance in Figure 5.6). The other participants could then click on the "slide control menu" button on a display to change slides.

Figure 5.11: SL Slideshows

Each group's display required a minimum of 4 slides (though most groups created more) that covered the following information:

- General planning: Title, group members, target group, general description of idea and objectives.
- The "big picture" of the podcast in their own words.
- The type(s) of materials they would need to produce their podcast.
- How they would assess the effectiveness of their podcast.

As part of this process it was necessary for the students to understand not just the language being used (in this case primarily English), but what also to understand the culture of the classrooms in the countries they came from. This was especially important since participants in this collaboration included representative of six different countries from 3 continents. Not only did this discussion include information regarding the difference between elementary schools between Spain, the U.S., Korea, Nicaragua, Taiwan, etc., but it also was necessary to discuss differences between younger and older students since some of the students in my course had never taught at the elementary level.

Prior to our final whole-group meeting of the collaboration, the groups provided me with their podcasts, which I published online. Everyone was sent the URL for the podcasts and asked to watch them before the final meeting (see Figure 5.12).

Figure 5.12: Final Meeting

Although the final meeting was primarily a social event with dancing and discussion, the students were also encouraged to comment on the podcasts produced by the other groups and to offer suggestions for changes. While this VWcollaboration project did not focus on some of the aspects of culture that have more often been examined, it was the nature of the interaction that made this collaboration both effective and productive because the students had a goal (to produce their podcasts) and partners they had met face-to-face (or in this case virtual face-to-virtual face).

Simulations—like cultural exchanges—are not a new phenomena. Many teachers have used them in their own real-life classrooms, having some students play the role of shoppers in a Mexican market, while others play the role of the Spanish-speaking shopkeepers. CALL programs like Rosetta Stone™ also often have sections that are meant to make users feel as if they are interacting in a market. However, as mentioned by Dooly (tbp), one key component in telecollaboration is that the language projects should be as authentic as possible, rather than language simulations in the traditional sense:

> This authenticity might lay in different domains of the learning activities (e.g. the project topic and context, the roles the students are required to take on, outside-the-classroom collaborators, the project output and/or the project audience). Corollary to [this focus on authenticity] is the notion of how the [collaboration] is designed, implemented and assessed so that distributed and shared knowledge-building (collaboration), learner-centred scaffolding and learner reflection are all part of the learning process.

The use of Virtual Worlds can help to address these very issues mentioned by Dooly because VW simulations can be taken to a much higher level of authenticity than is possible in any RL classroom, while simultaneously lowering student anxiety, as discussed earlier. While the simulations described below could easily be accomplished by a single class of students all in a computer lab together with their instructor, the use of the VW (rather than a traditional CALL-based simulation where the participants interact with the computer alone) also allows for the potential of involving another group of participants who are speakers of the language/culture under study. In that case, a simulation could be a VWcollaborative simulation between students studying German in Japan working with a group studying Japanese in the Germany (or any other combination of languages).

Marketplace Simulation

In Chapter 2 of this book, I briefly introduced a Synthetic Immersive Environment (SIE) called Croquelandia (Sykes, 2008). While that market environment is a very valuable education simulation it also required the use of profession programmers to create, and a good-sized budget to pay those programmers. That simulation also made use of bots integrated into the environment, designed to provide interactional opportunities for students by providing pre-programmed responses and/or requests for more information via a text-based interface. While this is certainly a very useful learning tool, this type of simulation does not fall under the umbrella of telecollaboration as defined in this book. By using an existing VW, I was able to create the European Marketplace simulation[21] (Figure 5.13) with a budget of less than $100 US and no outside programmers.

Figure 5.13: European Marketplace

While it would be possible to also program bots in SL (indeed some language researchers are working on such projects), this simulation was designed to be used by groups of students, in this case American

21 This simulation is available to any who may wish to use it. Please contact me via my SL name (Randall Renoir) for details.

students studying German, working with students from Germany studying English.

Fruit Stand	Meat and Fish	Bakery	Coffee Shop
Apples Bananas Cherries Oranges Lemons Grapefruit Pears Grapes Tomatoes Strawberries Raspberries Watermelon Melons	Steak Hamburger Roast Bacon Eggs Pork Pork chop Lamb Mutton Chicken Fish Crab Shrimp	Bread Bagels Pastry Donut Flour Wheat Whole Grain Cake Pie Cookies Croissant Muffin	Coffee Espresso Latte Mocha Tea Cream Sugar Cup Mug
Questions: Do you have any…? I would like a…. May I have a…? Can you tell me where to find…? Where is…? How much is…?		Misc. vocabulary areas: Weights Currency Sizes Colors Relative Directions Distances	

Table 5.1: Brief Sample of Marketplace Vocabulary

This simulation is set up to represent a fairly generic small European town market square, so it could also easily be used as a traditional market town in the UK, France, etc. with minor modifications. It consists of six main shops arranged around the square, 2 small vending stalls, a restaurant/pub (depending on the age of the participants!), and outdoor seating areas around the central fountain.

The shops include a fruit and vegetable store, a meat and seafood shop, a bakery, a coffee shop, and more. The square is meant to give the feel of actually shopping in a European market, and with the addition of two classes of students, with two different language backgrounds, the feeling (and noise level) would be even more authentic. In addition, this collaboration could also include a second simulation with the feel of an American marketplace. The key to this simulation is in the preparation of the participants. Prior to the marketplace activity, as seen in the very brief summary in Table 5.1, there is a great deal of vocabulary that might be discussed. Much of this vocabulary will be found in any lower-level language textbook, so I will not attempt to provide an exhaustive guide here. A simulation of this type is not meant to teach students vocabulary, but rather to reinforce it.

Figure 5.14: A Vendor Waiting for Customers

After preparing the students with the appropriate vocabulary, and finding a collaboration group, the students should be divided into two groups. In this case, the American students would be the shoppers (tourists visiting a German market town), and the native speakers of German would act as the vendors. (see Figure 5.14). If necessary, some students could act at the owner of two shops (busy entrepreneurs!). If there is enough time, students can cycle into the different roles, taking turns being the vendors. In keeping with a RL market, there should ideally be several shoppers per store to keep things busy, and to also let the students hear samples of what is happening before they make their own attempts at buying.

In order to make the interaction, and potentially the negotiation over prices, more authentic, I also developed two HUD devices to be used in the simulation. When given to a student and worn, the HUD will show up on the student's SL screen where it may be clicked as needed. The buyer's HUD (see Figure 5.15, top), in this case is stocked with Euros, and has eleven separate buttons representing the most common coins and bills for the currency.

Depending on the preferences of the teacher, there are two versions of the buyer's HUD that can be given to the students. The first version has unlimited money, so that they can go on a wild shopping spree. The second version, my own preference, has a limited supply of money, forcing the students to negotiate hard to get the best possible bargain. This HUD can be customized relatively easily to reflect other currencies as well. Once the buyer and seller agree on a price for an item (say, a perfectly ripe virtual apple for a mere 10 Euros), the buyer can click on that button, and then click on the shopkeeper's name in the list that comes up. The money will be given directly to the vendor's inventory, and he will have a message pop up telling him how much money he received. Once the shopkeeper receives his money, he can then use his own seller's HUD to give the buyer the requested item. The money that the HUD dispenses is not simply a number. The item that the seller receives in his inventory in this case would look like a very large 10 Euro bill.

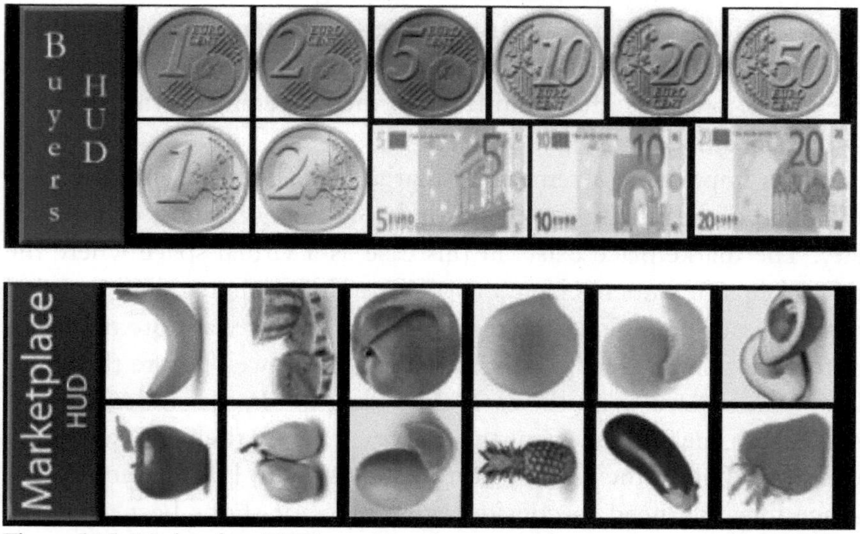

Figure 5.15: Marketplace HUDs

The seller's HUD (Figure 5.15, bottom), as might be guessed from the images on the buttons, is designed to be used by the vendor at the fruit stand and in used in the same way. If the buyer has purchased bananas and strawberries, the seller clicks on those two buttons, and then clicks on the buyer's name when it comes up. Once this is done, the two items will be delivered to the buyer's inventory directly. Once again, the buyer will have the "actual" virtual fruit in their inventory. I suppose if they get hungry while shopping they could even take the fruit out of their inventory and snack on it.

Since this simulation is designed so that a shopper can engage in negotiation over the price of an item with the shopkeeper, the teacher can decide how to set up the activity. I like to give each shopper a grocery list that is different, but that should cost roughly the same amount of money in RL. For example, shopper A's list may include 2 apples, 1 kilo of grapes, a loaf of bread, etc., while shopper B's list has 2 pears, 1 kilo of strawberries, some bagels, etc. This keeps both the shoppers and sellers on their virtual toes and makes them pay attention to the activity more closely. In addition, since they are trying to get the best deal, prizes can be given out for the best shoppers (most items for the least amount of money) and best vendors (most money made). To determine the winner, each participant will simply go to their inventory, and place all the items they bought and money they made onto the ground in front of them. Adding up the products and cash can be part of the activity.

It is important to remember that a Vcollaborative simulation of this type is meant to go well beyond rote memorization of vocabulary. The marketplace exists in this case as a virtual space where the two groups of students have the opportunity to interact in a way that is simply not possible in the regular classroom, or via more traditional forms of CMC. This collaboration can begin well before the simulation takes place. With the ease of building in SL, the students themselves can help to design the space, leading them to a deeper understanding of their own cultural environment. In designing such a space they will need to consider what types of shops best represent their own country, what products should be included, who the workers should be, and how they should interact with their customers (something that often varies greatly by culture and may lead to miscommunication), etc. In order to have an appropriate output for the project, the students may also be asked to produce a joint product requiring input from both groups—perhaps a guide for individuals who will be travelling to that other country and would like learn how to interact in a culturally appropriate manner while shopping. Of course, the types of simulations that could be designed are limited only by time and imagination.

While this HUD-based Marketplace Simulation is the only one I know of at this time in SL, there is are other groups at work on Edu-Nation (at the time of the printing of this book) on additional simulations to cover other situations like restaurants, hotels, etc. As with the simulation discussed above, these will be made freely available.

Second Life Tasks

As presented in Chapter 2, all VWs share a number of features, including a 3-D virtual environment, the use of avatars, real-time interactivity, 24-hour accessibility, persistence, and social space. However, some VWs, such as SL, also give users the ability to change the environment around them and, as discussed in Chapter 4, to create new objects in that world. These characteristics make VWs an ideal environment for students to engage in Task-Based Language Teaching (TBLT). According to Rod Ellis (2003), task should:

- include a workplan,
- have a "primary focus on meaning,"
- reflect real world communication,
- involve any of the four language skills,
- engage cognitive processes, and
- have a clearly defined communicative outcome.

Many of the foundations for TBLT were discussed in Chapter 3, including Dewey's Experiential Learning (1916), Vygotsky's Zone of Proximal Development (1978), and the Interaction Hypothesis (Long, 1980). As discussed earlier, all of these theories share the important idea that learners should be active participants in the education process rather than sitting passively in a traditional classroom. Given the hand-on nature of VWs like SL, there are no doubt thousands of possible tasks that students can engage in, ranging from the types of shopping simulations mentioned above, exploring sims and reporting back to the group on their potential for educational (or fun) activities, to creating some new product to actually sell in the VW. The key is that such tasks must be pedagogically sound rather than isolated fun:

> Just as teaching approaches are evolving, impulsed in part by the introduction of new technologies into classrooms across the world, so too have perspectives about well-established language teaching approaches. It is becoming increasingly more popular to consider 'tasks' as part of 'task sequences', that is,

> a carefully programmed sequence of tasks, sub-tasks, products and sub-products which are orchestrated by the teacher and which lead up to a relevant final product. This shifts the focus from small, decontextualised task-sequences designed by the teacher for presentation, practice and production of pre-selected linguistic forms to more embedded language learning that is more similar to project-based language learning. (Dooly, 2010: 286–287)

One of the tasks series that I have often used with my own students is collaborative building. The goal of this main task is simple—the students must build *something* with their partner(s). What they build, as long as they keep with the guidelines, will be entirely up to them. I have had students create items ranging from sofas, to abstract sculpture (at least I hope it was meant to be abstract) to a wonderfully creative glass-walled public bathroom. However, this task is actually a multi-step process:

1. Students build their *thing* with their partner(s).
2. As they build, they also create a full set of detailed instructions describing how they built it.
3. When complete, they give a copy of the item and the instructions to the teacher.
4. The teacher then gives a set of instructions to each group (one written by another group, and they follow those instructions to try to recreate what is described.
5. The original items and their recreations are compared side by side to see how similar they are.
6. The instructions are analyzed as a group to see why they worked (the original and recreation were very similar) or did not work.

Even with students who are familiar with SL, this task takes a minimum of two class periods to complete, though with students who are newer in SL, more ambitious in their builds, or more "linguistically challenged" it may take up to four classes to complete (this assume a 50-minute class). This activity does assume knowledge on the part of the instructor that goes beyond *basic* use of SL, but the skills needed here are not advanced.

While the goal of this task is to create their object, accomplishing this task with a partner will also require a great deal of authentic communication and negotiation since they must decide: *what* to create, how big it will be, what color and textures it will include, how each individual prim of the creation should be placed in comparison to the others, etc. As part of the pre-teaching for this task, vocabulary related to building, colors, textures, etc. should be discussed in class. In addition, it is useful to discuss how to write clear instructions as part of this activity (see Appendix A for information on writing instructions and for the task assignment). Completing this task also requires an area in which students have permissions to build things. If you do not own land in SL, simply do a search for sandbox in the SL interface and check the results. Sandboxes are places scattered throughout SL where anyone is allowed to build. Ideally, each group should be sent to a different sandbox so that they cannot see what the other groups are building. This makes the later steps in this activity much more challenging—and fun.

On the first day of the activity, the teacher should demonstrate basic building techniques in SL. This includes explaining what a prim is (many of these items discussed in Chapter 4), showing how to create objects, put on colors and textures (every avatar has some textures in the library folder in their inventory), and link things together (see information on those topics below and check the links at the end of Chapter 4 for tutorials).

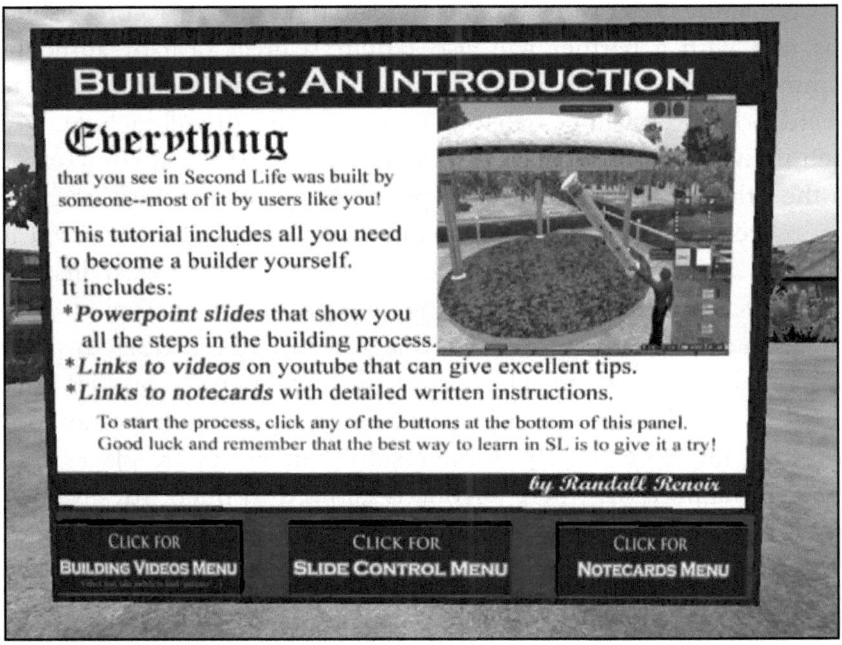

Figure 5.16: In-World Building Tutorial

Depending on the technical savvy of your students, they may be better at building that you are, or this first step may take an entire class. I have created a building tutorial tool in SL (see Figure 5.16) that include graphical descriptions of each step of the building process, links to instructional videos on YouTube, and notecards with additional detailed instructions[22].

After giving the task assignment (Appendix A), the students are put into groups and given the rest of the class to build their creation and make written instructions for another group to later recreate the item. If the groups have 3 individuals, I suggest one acts as the note taker, one as the builder, and one as the idea person. As mentioned before, groups should work in separate area in SL so they can't see what other groups are constructing. In the sample student build in

22 Message me in SL for a free copy—Randall Renoir.

Figure 5.17 (a comfy seating area) there a total of 18 prims and 6 textures used.

Figure 5.17: A Completed Building Task

In the next stage of the activity, the teacher should distribute copies of the building instructions created during the previous day's work to different groups. Each group will then take the instructions they have been given and attempt to recreate the original item. If the instructions are well written, this should take no more than 30 minutes. If the instructions are poorly written, this may take forever! In the last step, the class should all get together in the same spot in SL and the teacher should have each group put out its original object, and then the recreated objects should be set out next to the originals. This should continue until all the objects and their recreations are out. This section is usually good for some laughs, as some of the recreations are not even close to the originals. As homework, each person should then analyze why the instructions they created worked well or did not work well. They should also discuss why the instructions the received from another group worked or failed to work. This discussion can be carried over into the next class to improve upon their instructions.

Summary

This chapter began with a brief overview of settings in SL that have potential applications for language learning, followed by a number of pedagogical suggestions for using Virtual Worlds to enhance language learning. Beginning with a focus on telecollaboration and VW collaboration, and how SL can be used to facilitate group interaction, the chapter continued with an examination of a marketplace simulation. Finally, the possibility of performing collaborative task sequences in VWs was explored.

Suggested Readings

Written Resources

Aldrich, C. (2009). *Learning online with games, simulations, and virtual worlds*. San Francisco: Jossey-Bass.

Dooly, M. (ed.) (2008). *Telecollaborative language learning: A guidebook to moderating intercultural collaboration online*. Bern: Peter Lang.

O'Dowd, R. (2006). *Telecollaboration and the development of intercultural communicative competence*. Berlin: Langenscheidt.

Web-based Resources

Linden Lab Official: Linden Lab economic metric definitions (2011). Retrieved December 1, 2011 from <http://wiki.secondlife.com/wiki/Linden_Lab_Official:Linden_Lab_economic_metric_definitions>.

Linden Lab (2011). SL Education. Retrieved May 4, 2011 from <http://wiki.secondlife.com/wiki/Second_Life_Education>.

Chapter 6: Conclusion

This book has examined the history of Virtual Worlds, from their earliest days with multi-person text-based environments like Avatar and Empire—developed with the PLATO system—though their increasingly graphically-oriented descendents like MOOs and Lucasfilm's Habitat, and on to the colorful, interactive, 3D environments of today such as Club Penguin and Second Life. After examining the theory that is often used to support the role of VWs in learning and some of the research on CMC and VWs, Second Life was examined in more detail, both in terms of the interface of the VW and in relation to the users and their use of language. Finally, pedagogical environments and practice were introduced that might be useful for language learning in VWs.

As is often the case, the process of writing this book led me to a number of questions that I did not have time to answer, or for which no answers yet exist. In the section below I put forth my plea for the reader's help in answering questions in two areas that are currently in need of further research: pedagogical issues and questions related to a number of areas of sociolinguistics. Finally, I give my own thoughts about the direction that VWs may go in the future.

Future Research

While there is a rapidly growing body of research related to Virtual Worlds, as mentioned earlier most of this research has been in the form of case studies, and/or ethnographic in nature. As this type of study is one of my primary interests I value it highly, but there are certainly many other questions that remain to be answered, some of which require a more quantitative approach.

First, is the use of a VW more effective for the purpose of language learning than other forms or CMC and/or a RL classroom? We need research that examines this question, ideally providing quantifiable results. However, as any education researcher knows, these results often are made unclear by the number of confounding variables that can creep into educational studies. Perhaps Virtual Worlds are appropriate for some types of learning (e.g. I have found them to be excellent environments for virtual collaboration with groups of students located in other countries) but not effective for other types (e.g. grammar instruction). Whatever the case, there is a vast amount of research still to be done. Some of this research also needs to examine what RL pedagogical methods are best suited for use in VWs. While it is almost certain that the ancient Grammar-Translation method, with its focus on dictionary-based translations of existing texts, is most definitely not suited to VWs, a deeper examination of more recent methods and how they might be applied to VW use is needed.

Assuming that language teaching continues to take place in VWs—and I would argue that it most certainly should—another question is how we should evaluate students in this environment or if we should evaluate them at all. Evaluating students that you cannot see (at least in RL) is a challenge, but online evaluation is now a well-established field. The challenge in VWs is to develop forms of evaluation that are best suited to the strengths of those environments. Research will show us what those forms should be.

Beyond pedagogical research, there is also a burgeoning field of sociolinguistic research taking place in VWs. However, once again, this process has barely begun. This list below is a by-no-means-exhaustive selection of sociolinguistics-related topics in need of further research in VWs and in many cases in the larger field of CMC as well. All of these areas need further study in English, and any other language being used in VWs.

Gender and Language: While this area has been examined to some extent, the complexity of gender in Virtual Worlds makes it an area with many dissertations worth of research still to accomplish. How many RL men are women in SL? Are they always women in SL or only part of the time? As women in SL, do they use the same patterns of communication as RL women who exist as SL female avatars, or do they "speak" like men dressed as women? Do women and men who exist as neutral SL avatars (e.g. some genderless robot or vehicle shapes) still communicate the same way, or does their new look have an effect on their language?

Accommodation: Is accommodation in a virtual world exhibited in the same way as in the RW? In a diverse world such as Second Life, where speakers of so many languages interact, both in text and oral communication, this becomes a very complex question, well worthy of further research.

Back channeling: Is there more or less back channeling in a VW in comparison to RL? Is it done differently? This is an especially interesting area since the amount of non-verbal back channeling possible in virtual worlds is increasing through the use of HUDs designed for non-verbal communication that include gestures like nods, winks, yawns, etc.

Floor: How do speakers keep their turn or take the floor in virtual conversations? How does this differ between text-based and oral chat in VWs? What role, if any, does non-verbal communication play in this process in VWs in comparison to RL?

Code-switching: How is code switching done in multilingual virtual environments (it is definitely done since I've both witnessed it and engaged in code-switching in SL myself)?

Communities of Practice: Given the fact that all new members of virtual environments are newbies, how do they become members of the community, both culturally and linguistically? Since VWs are relatively new creations, this is an area of research full of brand new CoPs available for study.

Speech Acts: This area has been extensively studied for a number of languages in RL environments, but has been examined much less for CMC communication and the field is wide open in VWs. How are speech acts like requests, refusals, invitations, etc. made in VWs versus other forms of CMC or in RL? Does relative status play the same role in VW speech acts as it does in RL?

The topics related to sociolinguistics research mentioned immediately above only scratch the surface of research that needs to be accomplished. Any student or researcher doing work in this area can look at any sociolinguistics topic studied in RL and find that little or no work has been done in that area for VWs.

Future Directions of VWs

> The people I knew who actually knew anything about computers when I'd try to talk to them about it, about idea I would have for..stories, they would always say 'Ohhh, you know, forget it. That's never gonna happen.' For instance, they'd say 'there's not enough bandwidth.' And when Neuromancer came out [in 1984] I heard that a lot. They said 'this is ridiculous. There's never going to be enough bandwidth.' I didn't even know what bandwidth was, but whatever it was I knew that there was gonna be a whole lot more of it real soon now, which proved to be the case. (Gibson, 2007)

Anyone who has seen old black-and-white science fiction movies from the 1950s or early TV series like Star Trek knows that accurately predicting the future can be extremely difficult. In some cases we are still waiting for technology to catch up with fiction. Star Trek teleporters and Warp Drives are not yet in the realm of science, and many would argue that they never will be. On the other hand, other elements like Star Trek communicators have already been surpassed by modern technology like cellular phones—technology that is much smaller than the Star Trek versions, and can also include video communication, thousands of Apps, entertainment, GPS, and much more. As mentioned by Gibson in the 2007 PBS interview quoted above, this was also the case with Neuromancer, at least in some respects. As someone who was amazed at how fast I was able to access information on the Internet on my first computer (equipped with a 14.4 kb/s dial up modem), my connection speed of today (normally over 20mb/s) was simply beyond my imagining.

Although Virtual Worlds like Second Life are still not at the level of the cyberspace depicted in Gibson's book in some respects (not yet totally immersive for all senses), their potential—as computers and bandwidth expand and evolve—continues to increase exponentially. Given their popularity, it appears likely (at the very least) that Virtual Worlds will continue to exist for some time into the future. In terms of potential changes to these environments, continued advances in both computer graphics and Internet connection speeds make it likely that these worlds will continue to become increasingly realistic in terms of what is seen on the screen and that they will also function more smoothly. This means that their sense of reality for students will continue to increase, making interactions in Virtual Worlds even more authentic and, with increased speeds, smoother.

With advances in translation software and in-world translation devices, it is also possible that language will become a non-issue in terms of virtual communication. While the translation devices currently available online and in VWs are still fairly rudimentary (some might say horrible), avatars are using them already to engage in successful communication (another possible research topic!), albeit at a fairly basic level (they are not yet the universal translators promised by Star Trek). This may have profound implications in the future for both language learning and teaching—I am hoping it will not put we language teachers out of business.

The way in which users interact with VWs world is also continuing to evolve, with devices like the X-box Kinect™ showing that it is now easily possible to interface with a computer-based environment with no use of a computer keyboard whatsoever. It may soon be possible to reach towards a computer screen to pluck an apple from a tree in SL or to flap your arms while sitting at your desk to fly across a sim (best to not do that one in a public computer lab).

I am confident about several points related to the questions I have laid out above. In five or ten years, I am certain that a number of the pedagogical and sociolinguistics questions I asked above will be at the very least partially answered. I am also confident that the predictions I made above—in keeping with the predictions made in those science fiction movies—will be partially right and partially wildly wrong. Check back with me in 2020 and tell me which were on track.

Appendix: Instructions for Building Task

While writing instructions may not seem to be directly connected to the building task for the students, this is a skill that is applicable to a number of fields in education and business. Anyone who has tried to put together a bookcase that has 135 pieces, and ended up with 15 "spare" items and a very shaky bookcase knows that writing clear instructions—whether for putting together a bookcase, programming a computer, or building an item in SL—is an important skill.

Writing Instructions

Although the exact way that instructions are written may vary depending on the purpose of the instruction (e.g., baking a cake versus installing RAM on a computer) and the people they are written for (e.g., children versus adults), most instructions share some elements in common, as shown below:

1. A Clear Title: this should explain: What you are writing about, why you are writing.
2. Good Organization: This gives your readers a roadmap to follow.
3. Introduction: The topic you will discuss, your reasons for writing, the number of steps that it will take.
4. Body: The steps to follow, clear explanation, graphics (if needed). If you do use graphics:

Could include:	Should be:
Drawings	simple and clear
Photos	labeled

5. Conclusion.
6. Instructions for how to get help if your reader cannot follow the instructions.
7. An Easy to follow Style: Number your steps instead of using bullets, use highlighting techniques (e.g., Boldface, italics, different fonts, size, color, etc.), limit the amount of information in each step.

TOO MUCH INFORMATION
First, create the first prim for the artwork. To create the prim, first turn on your computer and log in. After you finish logging in, wait for your computer to warm up and then turn on the screen. Find your "programs" menu and find SL, and then start SL.

RIGHT AMOUNT OF INFORMATION
Create the first prim by clicking on the "build" button in SL, and then clicking on the cube shape in the window that comes up.

Other Style Tips

Develop each point thoroughly, use short words and phrases, begin your steps with verbs—use imperative:
- E.g., Move the wall 2 meters to the right.
- Personalize your text.
- E.g., Next, you should….

Word Choice

Choose the words you use carefully so that your readers will understand exactly what you want them to do. Some examples for a building assignment might include:

Building Vocabulary:

Making & Selecting	Changing	Movement	Prepositions of location	Adjectives
Create	Expand	Move	On	Long
Build	Shrink	Lift	In	Short
Rezz	Stretch	Raise	Under	Small
Duplicate		Lower	Over	Large
	Color	Slide	Next to	Square
Click	Texturize	Place	Behind	Round
Right-click		Push	Between	Flat
Select	Attach	Pull	In front of	Thin
Edit	Link	Put		Thick
Choose	Connect	Rotate		

Choose your prepositions of location with care. If you use the wrong one in the instructions it could be very bad! ;-)

Final Point

Don't rely on the X,Y,Z coordinates in SL when making directions. If someone follows your directions at another region in SL, those will have no meaning!

Building Task

Follow the instructions below to complete the building task assignment. Remember, this is a GROUP project, so everyone must participate!

Instructions are one very important genre of writing. Instructions may include something as simple as following a recipe to cook a cake or, perhaps in a future career, writing instructions or a technical manual telling your customers how to put together a piece of furniture, a computer, etc. Maybe some of you have tried to make something with some instructions that were NOT well written. It is very difficult and frustrating!

This assignment will have you:
1. Build something in a group, AND
2. Make instructions so that another group can build the same thing.

In Second Life, everything you see is made up of two basic things: objects and textures.

OBJECTS are basic shapes like cubes, rectangles, spheres, etc. For most things (like chair, a house, a sculpture, etc.) many individual objects are "linked" together.

TEXTURES give an object a different look (like wood, stone, glass, different colors, etc.).

Instructions

1. Create something in Second Life. Do this by clicking on the "Build" button at the bottom of your SL screen. A new window will pop up and allow you to create new objects in SL (these include basic geometric shapes such as cubes, spheres, cylinders, cones, etc.). This window will also let you change the size and shape of the objects you create. Everything you see in SL (other than avatars) is built using these basic shapes. Although the scope of this article does not allow for a detailed building tutorial, the building tutorial tool mentioned earlier gives full instructions. After you build your creation, add textures/colors however you'd like. The final creation should be "something" but your group will decide what that will be. It could be a building, a piece of furniture, a crazy piece of art—anything you decide. Use your imagination! Your group must discuss what you want to build. Negotiate as you go!
2. As you make the creation, have at least one person in your group take careful notes about HOW you are making it (This is VERY important).

3. Your group must now make a complete and detailed set of instructions on a notecard so that another group will be able to make EXACTLY the same thing you did.

Rules

A. You must use at least 5 objects to make your final creation
B. You must use at least 3 colors and/or textures

When making your instructions carefully consider:
- Which objects to use.
- How to position and rotate those objects.
- How to put on the textures (which sides of which objects, is the texture repeated, is it partially transparent? etc.).

Goal

After 50 minutes you should have:
1. Your final creation by your group.
2. A notecard with complete instructions so that another group can make exactly the same object

Put a copy of the final creation and the notecard in a folder and give the folder to me in SL (name the folder "Build by *your names here*").

In the next class, another group will be given your instructions and they will try to recreate your item. After that, we'll compare the final creation you made with the one made by the group that followed your instructions!

Bibliography

Absalom, M. & Marden, M. P. (2004). Email communication and language learning at university- an Australian case study. *Computer Assisted Language Learning, 17*(3–4), 403–440.

ActiveWorlds. (2010). *Active Worlds content guidelines.* Retrieved January 3, 2010, from <http://www.activeworlds.com/community/terms.asp>.

Aldrich, C. (2009). *The complete guide to simulations & serious games: How the most valuable content will be created in the age beyond Gutenberg to Google.* San Francisco: Pfeiffer.

Aldrich, C. (2009). *Learning online with games, simulations, and virtual worlds: Strategies for online instruction.* San Francisco: Jossey-Bass.

Anderson, T. & Elloumi, F. (2004). *Theory and practice of online Learning.* Retrieved March 15, 2006 from <http://cde.athabascau.ca/online_book/index. html>.

Antonacci, D. M. & Modaress, N. (2005). *Second Life: The educational possibilities of a massively multiplayer virtual world (MMVW).* Paper presented at the EDUCAUSE Southwest Regional Conference. Retrieved December 16, 2010 from <http://www.educause.edu/ LibraryDetailPage/666?ID=SWR0552>.

Backer, J. A. (1999). *Multi-User Domain Object Oriented (MOO) as a High School procedure for foreign language acquisition* (Unpublished doctoral dissertation). Nova Southeastern University.

Ball, S. & Pearce, R. (2009). Inclusion benefits and barriers of "once removed" participation. In C. Wankel & J. Kingsley (Eds.), *Higher education in virtual worlds: Teaching and learning in Second Life* (pp. 47–63). Bingley: Emerald.

Ballou, E. A. G. (2002). *Teaching language and culture with computer-mediated communications technologies.* (Unpublished doctoral dissertation). University of Massachusetts Amherst.

Banakou, D., Chorianopoulos, K., & Anagnostou, K. (2009). *Avatars' appearance and social behavior in online virtual worlds.* Paper presented at the 13th Panhellenic Conference on Informatics. Retrieved Feb 17, 2010 from <http://.computer.org/portal/web/csdl/doi/10.1109/PCI.2009.9>.

Bani, M., Genovesi, F., Ciregia, E., Piscioneri, F., Rapisarda, B., Salvatori, E., et al. (2009). Learning by creating historical buildings. In J. Molka-Danielsen & M. Deutschmann (Eds.), *Learning and teaching in the virtual world of Second Life* (pp. 125–144). Trondhein: Tapir Academic Press.

Barab, S. A., Hay, K. E., Barnet, M., & Squire, K. (2001). Constructing virtual worlds: Tracing the historical development of learner practices. *Cognition and Instruction, 19*(1), 47–94.

Barnes, S. B. (2003). *Computer-mediated communication: human-to-human communication across the Internet.* Boston, MA: Pearson Education.

Bearden, R. J. (2003). *Chatting in a foreign language: An interactional study of oral vs. computer-assisted discussion in native speaker and non-native learner dyads.* (Unpublished doctoral dissertation). The University of Texas at Austin.

Beauvois, M. H. & Eledge, J. (1995). Personality types and megabytes: student attitudes toward computer mediated communication (CMC) in the language classroom. *CALICO Journal, 13*(2&3), 27–45.

Belcher, D. (1999). Authentic interaction in a virtual classroom: Leveling the playing field in a graduate seminar. *Computers and Composition, 16*, 253–267.

Beli, N., Noteborn, G. & de Ruyter, K. (2009). Cross-world branding—One world is not enough. In C. Wankel & J. Kingsley (Eds.), *Higher education in virtual worlds: Teaching and learning in Second Life* (pp. 115–139). Bingley: Emerald.

Bell, M. W., Castronova, E. & Wagner, G. G. (2009). *Surveying the virtual world: A large scale survey in Second Life using the virtual data collection interface (VDCI).* Berlin: Council for social and economic data.

Belz, J. A. & Kinginger, C. (2002). The cross-linguistics development of address form use in telecollaborative language learning: Two case studies. *Canadian Modern Language Review/Revue Canadienne des langues vivant, 59*(2), 189–214.

Belz, J. A. & Kinginger, C. (2003). Discourse options and the development of pragmatic competence by classroom learners of German: The case of address forms. *Language Learning 53*(4), 591–647.

Benton, R. A. (1996). Making the medium the message: using electronic bulletin board system for promoting and revitalizing Maori. In M. Warschauer (Ed.), *Telecollaboration in foreign language learning* (pp. 187–204). Honolulu: University of Hawaii Press.

Biesenbach-Lucas, S. & Weasenforth, D. (2001). E-mail and word processing in the ESL classroom: How the medium affects the message. *Language, Learning & Technology, 5*(1), 135.

Braine, G. (1997). Beyond word processing: Networked computers in ESL writing classes. *Computers and Composition, 14*, 45–58.

Bricken, M. (1991). Virtual reality learning environments: Potentials and challenges. *Computer Graphics, 25*(3), 178–184.

Broadribb, S., Peachey, A., Carter, C. & Westrap, F. (2009). Using Second Life at the Open University: How virtual worlds can facilitate learning for staff and students. In C. Wankel & J. Kingsley (Eds.), *Higher education in virtual worlds: Teaching and learning in Second Life* (pp. 203–219). Bingley: Emerald.

Bronack, S., Riedl, R. & Tashner, J. (2006). Learning in the zone: A social constructivist framework for distance education in a 3-dimensional virtual world. *Interactive Learning Environments, 14*(3), 219–232.

Brown, B. & Bell, M. (2004). *CSCW at play: 'There' as a collaborative virtual environment.* Paper presented at the 2004 ACM Conference on Computer Supported Cooperative Work, Chicago, Illinois.

Bystrom, K.-E. & Barfield, W. (1999). Collaborative task performance for learning using a virtual world. *Presence, 8*(4), 435–448.

Cameron, J. (Writer). (2009). *Avatar* [Film]. U.S.: 20th Century Fox.

Chapelle, C. A. (2001). Innovative language learning: Achieving the vision. *ReCALL, 13*(1), 3–14.

Childress, M. D. & Braswell, R. (2006). Using massively multiplayer online role-playing games for online learning. *Distance Education, 27*(2), 187–196.

Chun, D. (1994). Using computer networking to facilitate the acquisition of interactive competence. *System, 22*(1), 17–31.

Churchill, E. F. & Snowdon, D. (1998). Collaborative virtual environments: An introductory review of issues and systems. *Virtual Reality, 3*, 3–15.

ClubPenguin (2010, January 21, 2010). *Player safety.* Retrieved February 2, 2010 from <http://www.clubpenguin.com/parents/player_safety.htm>.

Cooke-Plagwitz, J. (2008). New directions in CALL: An objective introduction to Second Life. *CALICO Journal, 25*(3), 547–557.

Crook, C. (1994). *Computers and the collaborative experience of learning.* New York: Routledge.

Crystal, D. (2001). *Language and the Internet.* Cambridge: Cambridge Press.

Cziko, G. A. & Park, S. (2003). Internet audio communication for second language learning: a comparative review of six programs. *Language learning & Technology, 7*(1), 15–27.

Dewey, J. (1916). *Democracy and education.* New York: The Macmillan Company.

Dewey, J. (1939). *Experience and education.* New York: The Macmillan Company.

Dickey, M. D. (1999). *3D virtual worlds and learning: An analysis of the impact of design affordances and limitations in Active Worlds, Blaxxun Interactive, and OnLive! Traveler; and a study of the implepmentation of Active Worlds for formal and information education* (Unpublished doctoral dissertation). The Ohio State University, Columbus.

Dickey, M. D. (2005). Three-dimensional virtual worlds and distance learning: Two case studies of Active Worlds as a medium for distance education. *British Journal of Educational Technology, 36*(3), 439–451.

Dillenbourg, P., Schneider, D. & Synteta, P. (2002). *Virtual learning environments.* Paper presented at the 3rd Hellenic Conference "information & communication technologies in education".

Dooly, M. (ed.) (2008). *Telecollaborative language learning: A guidebook to moderating intercultural collaboration online.* Bern: Peter Lang.

Dooly, M. (2010). Teacher 2.0. In S. Guth & F. Helm (Eds), *Telecollaboration 2.0. Language, literacies and intercultural learning in the 21st century* (pp. 277–303). Bern: Peter Lang.

Dooly, M. (tbp 2011). Promoting competency-based language teaching through project-based language learning. In M. Peréz (Ed.), *Competency-based language teaching in higher education, AILA Applied Linguistics Series.* Amsterdam: John Benjamins.

Doughty, C. J. (2000). Negotiating the L2 linguistic environment. *University of Hawai'i working papers in ESL* (pp. 47–83). Manoa: University of Hawai'i.

Dubner, S. L. (2007, February 12). *Philip Rosedale answers your Second Life questions.* Retrieved February 2, 2008 from <http://freakonomics.blogs.nytimes.com/2007/ 12/13/philip-rosedale-answers-your-second-life-questions/>.

Ducate, L. C. (2003). *Culture, communication, community: Co-constructing knowledge and cultural images through computer-mediated communication.* (Unpublished doctoral dissertation). The University of Texas at Austin.

Edlinger, M. (2008). *Interaction in virtual worlds: Concepts, applications and restrictions.* Saarbrüken: VDM.

Egbert, J. & Hanson-Smith, E. (Eds.) (1999). *CALL environments: Research, practice, and critical issues.* Alexandria, Virginia: Teachers of English to Speakers of Other Languages.

Egbert, J., Chao, C.-C. & Hanson-Smith, E. (2005). Computer-enhanced language learning environments: an overview. In J. Egbert, J. & Petrie, G. M. (Eds.), *CALL research perspectives* (pp. 1–13). Mahwah, NJ: Lawrence Erlbaum Associates.

Ellis, A. E. (2003). Personality type and participation in networked learning environments. *Educational Media International, 40*(1/2), 101–114.

Ellis, R. (1991). *The Interaction Hypothesis: A critical evaluation.* Paper presented at the Regional Language Centre Seminar.

Ellis, R. (1997). *SLA research and language teaching.* Oxford: Oxford University Press.

Faivre, S. (2009). *ESL online, a curriculum project: How to wire students to today's educational grid using Second Life and other Internet resources* (Unpublished M.A. Thesis). The University of Illinois at Urbana-Champaign.

Fanderclai, T. L. (1995). MUDs in education: New environment, new pedagogies. *Computer-Mediated Communication Magazine, 2*, 8–10.

Fedderholdt, K. (2001). An Email Exchange Project between Non-Native Speakers of English. *ELT Journal, 55*(3), 273–280.

Fotos, S. & Browne, C. (Eds.) (2004). *New perspectives on CALL for second language classrooms.* Mahwah, NJ: Lawrence Erlbaum Associates.

Freiermuth, M. R. (2001). *Features of electronic synchronous communication: A comparative analysis of online chat, spoken and written texts* (Unpublished doctoral dissertation). Oklahoma State University.

Freiermuth, M. R. (2001). Native speakers or nonnative speakers: Who has the floor? Online and face-to-face interaction in culturally mixed small groups. *Computer Assisted Language Learning, 14*(2), 169–199.

Freiermuth, M. R. (2002). Internet Chat: Collaborating and Learning via E-Conversations. *TESOL Journal, 11*(3), 36–40.

Furman, N., Goldberg, D. & Lusin, N. (2007). *Enrollments in Languages Other Than English in United States Institutions of Higher Education, Fall 2006*: Modern Language Association of America.

Garau, M., Slater, M., Bee, S. & Sasse, M. A. (2001). *The impact of eye gaze on communication using humanoid avatars.* Paper presented at the Conference on Human Factors in Computing Systems, Seattle.

Gerson, S. & Gerson, S. (1993). *Technical writing: Process and product.* Upper Saddle River, NJ: Prentice Hall.

Gibson, W. (1984). *Neuromancer.* New York: Ace Books.

Gronstedt, A. (2007). Second Life produces real training results: The 3-D web world is slowly becoming part of the training industry. *Training and Development*, 44–49.

Gu, N., Gul, L. F., Williams, A. & Nakapan, W. (2009). Second Life—A context for design learning. In C. Wankel & J. Kingsley (Eds.), *Higher education in virtual worlds: Teaching and learning in Second Life* (pp. 159–180). Bingley: Emerald.

Guilherme, M. (2000). Intercultural competence. In M. Byram (Ed.), *Routledge encylopaedia of language teaching and learning* (pp. 78–81). London: Routledge.

Habbo (2010). *Habbo Hotel—Where else?* Retrieved February 6, 2010 from <http://www.sulake.com/habbo>.

Hampel, R. & Hauck, M. (2004). Towards an effective use of audio conferencing in distance language courses. *Language learning & Technology, 8*(1), 66–82.

Hanna, B. & de Nooy, J. (2003). A funny thing happened on the way to the forum: Electronic discussion and foreign language learning. *Language Learning & Technology, 7*(1), 71–85.

Hanna, B. E. & Nooy, J. D. (2004). Negotiating cross-cultural difference in electronic discussion. *Multilingua, 23*, 257–281.

Harris, K. (1995). Internet in the classroom: A gold mine or a lot of hype? *CALL Review: The Journal of the IATEFL Computer Special Interest Group.* Retrieved September 9, 2009 from <http://www.iatefl.org/calrevnv. html>.

Henri, F. & Pudelko, B. (2003). Understanding and analysing activity and learning in virtual communities. *Journal of Computer Assisted Language Learning, 19*, 474–487.

Hofsøy, M. B. (2001). *Network-based EFL: motivational aspects of using networked computers in the EFL classroom* (Unpublished M.A. Thesis). University of Bergen.

International Civil Avilation Organization (2011). *ICAO promotes aviation safety by endorsing English language testing.* Retrieved October 22, 2011 from: <http://www2.icao.int/en/NewsRoom/Lists /News/DispForm.aspx?ID=58>.

Jæger, B. R. & Helghein, B. (2009). Role play study in a purchase management class. In J. Molka-Danielsen & M. Deutschmann (Eds.), *Learning and teaching in the virtual world of Second Life* (pp. 115–123). Trondheim: Tapir Academic Press.

Jarmon, L., Traphagan, T., Mayrath, M. & Trivedi, A. (2009). Virtual world teaching, experiential learning and assessment: An interdisciplinary communication course in Second Life. *Computers & Education, 53*, 169–182.

Jarmon, L., Watanabe Traphagan, T., Traphagan, J. W. & Jones Eaton, L. (2009). Aging, lifelong learning, and the virtual world of Second Life. In C. Wankel & J. Kingsley (Eds.), *Higher education in virtual worlds: Teaching and learning in Second Life* (pp. 221–242). Bingley: Emerald.

Kamhi-Stein, L. D. (2000). Looking to the future of TESOL teacher education: web-based bulletin board discussion in a methods course. *TESOL Quarterly, 34*(3), 423–455.

Kapp, K. & O'Driscoll, T. (2010). *Learning in 3D: Adding a new dimension to enterprise learning and collaboration.* San Francisco: Pfeiffer.

Kelm, O. R. (1996). The application of computer networking in foreign language education: focusing on principles of second language acquisition. In M. Warschauer (Ed.), *Telecollaboration in Foreign Language Learning* (pp. 19–28). Honolulu: University of Hawaii Press.

Kern, R. (1995). Restructuring classroom interaction with networked computers: effects on quantity and characteristics of language production. *The Modern Language Journal, 79*(4), 457–476.

Kitade, K. (2006). The negotiation model in asynchromous computer-mediated communication (CMC): Negotiation in task-based email exchanges. *CALICO Journal, 23*(2), 319–348.

Ki-hong, K. (2004). New forms of online communication spell end of email era in Korea. *Digital Chosumnilbo (English Edition).* Retrieved January 16, 2006, from <http://english.chosun.com/w21data/html/news/200411/200411280034.html>.

Kolb, D. A. (1984). *Experiential Learning: Experience as the source of learning and development.* Upper Saddle River, NJ: Prentice Hall.

Kötter, M. (2001). Developing distance language learners' interactive competence - can synchronous audio do the trick? *International Jl. of Educational Telecommunications, 7*(4), 327–353.

Kötter, M. (2001). MOOrituri te salutant? Language learning through MOO-based synchronous exchanges between learner tandems. *Computer Assisted Language Learning, 14*(3–4), 289–304.

Kötter, M., Shield, L. & Stevens, A. (1999). Real-time audio and email for fluency: promoting distance language learners' aural and oral skills via the internet. *ReCALL, 11*(2), 55–60.

Horowitz, A., Jefferies, R., Kitsis, E., Klugman, B., Lisberger, S., and Sternthal, L. (Writers). (2010) *Tron: Legacy* [film]. Walt Disney.

Krashen, S. (1985). *The input hypothesis: issues and implications.* New York: Longman.

KZERO (2010). *KZERO Worldwide.* Retrieved February 2, 2010, from <http://www.kzero.co.uk/#>.

Lamy, M.N. (2004). Oral conversations online: redefining oral competence in synchronous environments. *ReCALL, 16*, 520–538.

Lamy, M-N. & Goodfellow, R. (2010). Telecollaboration and Learning 2.0. In S. Guth & F. Helm (Eds.), *Telecollaboration 2.0. Language, literacies and intercultural learning in the 21st century,* Telecollaboration in Education Series (pp. 107–138). Bern: Peter Lang.

Levy, M. (1997). *Computer-Assisted Language Learning: context and conceptualization.* Oxford: Oxford University Press.

Lewin, K. (1951). *Field theory in social sciences.* New York: Harper & Row.

Lisberger, S. (Writer) (1982). *Tron* [film]: Walt Disney.

Long, M. H. (1980). *Input, interaction and second language acquisition* (Unpublished doctoral dissertation). UCLA.

Long, M. H. (1981). The input hypothesis: issues and implications. *Annals of the New York Academy of Sciences, 379*, 259–278.

Long, M. H. (1983). Native speaker/non-native speaker conversation and the negotiation of comprehensible input. *Applied Linguistics, 4*(2), 126–141.

Love, E., Ross, S. C. & Wilhelm, W. (2009). Opportunities and challenges for business education in Second Life. In C. Wankel & J. Kingsley (Eds.), *Higher education in virtual worlds: Teaching and learning in Second Life* (pp. 65–82). Bingley: Emerald.

Markel, M. (2001). *Technical Communication.* Boston: Bedford/St. Martin's.

May, P. (2010). *Virtually dead: A mystery.* Scottsdale, AZ: Poisoned Pen Press.

McAleer Balkun, M., Zedeck, M. & Trotta, H. (2009). Literary analysis as serious play in Second Life. In C. Wankel & J. Kingsley (Eds.), *Higher education in virtual worlds: Teaching and learning in Second Life* (pp. 141–157). Bingley: Emerald.

Meskill, C. & Anthony, N. (2004). Teaching and Learning with Telecommunications: Instructional Discourse in a Hybrid Russian Class. *Journal of Educational Technology Systems, 33*(2), 103–119.

Meskill, C. & Anthony, N. (2005). Foreign language learning with CMC: forms of online instructional discourse in a hybrid Russian class. *System, 33*, 89–105.

Mikropoulos, T., Chalkidis, A., Katsikis, A. & Emvalotis, A. (1998). Students' attitudes towards educational virtual environments. *Education and Information Technologies, 3*, 137–148.

mmohut (2010). *mmohut: Free online MMORPG and MMO games.* Retrieved January 16, 2010 from <http:// mmohut.com>.

mmorpg.com (2010). *mmorpg.* Retrieved January 11, 2010 from <http://.mmorpg.com/>.

Molka-Danielsen, J. & Deutschmann, M. (Eds.). (2009). *Learning and teaching in the virtual world of Second Life.* Trondheim: Tapir Academic Press.

Morningstar, C. & Farmer, F. (2001). Habitat: Reports from an online community. In Frenkel, J. (Ed.), *True names and the opening of the cyberspace frontier* (pp. 239–330). New York: TOR.

Mostow, J. (Writer) (2009). *Surrogates* [film]: Touchstone Pictures.

Murray, D. E. (2000). Protean communication: the language of computer-mediated communication. *TESOL Quarterly, 34*(3), 397–421.

Murray, G. L. & Bollinger, D. J. (2001). Developing Cross-Cultural Awareness: Learning through the Experiences of Others. *TESL Canada Journal, 19*(1), 62–72.

Nunan, D. (2004). *Task-based language teaching*. Cambridge: Cambridge University Press.

O'Dowd, R. (2000). Intercultural learning via videoconferencing: a pilot exchange project. *ReCALL, 12*(1), 49–61.

O'Dowd, R. (2001). In search of a truly global network: the opportunities and challenges of on-line intercultural. *CALL-EJ Online, 3*(1).

O'Dowd, R. (2003). Understanding the "other side": intercultural learning in a Spanish-English e-mail exchange. *Language learning & Technology, 7*(2), 118–144.

O'Dowd, R. (2004). *Network-based language teaching and the development of intercultural communicative competence.* University Duisburg-Essen.

O'Dowd, R. (2006). *Telecollaboration and the development of intercultural communicative competence.* München: Langenscheidt.

Palfrey, J. & Gasser, U. (2008). *Born digital: Understanding the first generation of digital natives.* New York: Basic Books.

Paver, J. A. (2003). *The zone of proximal development in an online ESL composition course* (Unpublished doctoral dissertation). University of Nevada, Las Vegas.

Pellettieri, J. (2000). Negotiation in cyberspace: The role of chatting in the developing of grammatical competence. In M. Warschauer & R. Kern (Eds.), *Network-based language teaching: Concepts and practice* (pp. 59–86). Cambridge, UK: Cambridge University Press.

Perez, L. C. (2003). Foreign language productivity in synchronous versus asynchronous computer-mediated communication. *CALICO Journal, 21*(1), 89–104.

Peterson, M. (2001). MOOs and second language acquisition: Towards a rationale for MOO-based learning. *Computer Assisted Language Learning 14*(5), 443–459.

Pica, T. (1987). Second language acquisition, social interaction and the classroom. *Applied Linguistics, 8*, 1–25.

Price, S. & Rogers, Y. (2004). Let's get physical: The learning benefits of interacting in digitally augmented physical spaces. *Computers and Education, 43*, 137–151.

Reid, E. (1994). *Cultural formations in text-based virtual realities* (Unpublished M.A. Thesis). University of Melbourne.

Rheingold, H. (1991). *Virtual reality.* New York: Simon & Schuster.

Rheingold, H. (1993). A slice of life in my virtual community. In L. M. Harasim (Ed.), *Global networks: Computers and international communication* (pp. 57–80). Cambridge: MIT Press.

Robbins, S. & Bell, M. (2008). *Second Life for dummies.* Indianapolis: Wiley.

Roussou (2004). Learning by doing and learning through play: An exploration of interactivity in virtual environments for children. *AMC Computers in Entertainment, 2*(1), 1–23.

Sadler, R. W. (2007). Computer-mediated communication and a cautionary tale of two cities. *CALICO Journal, 25*(1), 11–30.

Sadler, R. & Eröz, B. (2008). Training language teachers in the theoretical and practical applications of message boards. In M. Dooly (Ed.), *New Technologies.* (pp. 187–199). Newcastle upon Tyne: Cambridge Scholars Press.

Sadler, R. (2009). *Strange new worlds: Opportunities and cautions in virtual world research.* Keynote Address at Illinois Language and Linguistics Society 1: Language Online, University of Illinois at Urbana-Champaign, Urbana, IL.

Sadler, R. (2009). Can you build this? Virtual construction for language learning in Second Life. In L. Stone & C. Wilson-Duff (Eds.), *Task-based III: Expanding the range of tasks with online resources* (pp. 212–226). IALT.

Samsonov, P. V. (2001). *Effectiveness of teaching a part of a foreign language course through computer-mediated communication as perceived by the students of Texas A&M University and military reservists: A case study* (Unpublished doctoral dissertation). Texas A&M University.

Sant, T. (2009). Performance in Second Life: Some possibilities for learning and teaching. In J. Molka-Danielsen & M. Deutschmann (Eds.), *Learning and teaching in the virtual world of Second Life* (pp. 145–166). Trondheim: Tapir Academic Press.

Schroeder, R. (Ed.) (2002). *The social life of avatars: Presence and interaction in shared virtual environments.* London: Springer.

Schrooten, W. (2006). Task-based language teaching and ICT: Developing and assessing interactive multimedia for task-based language teaching. In K. Van den Branden (Ed.), *Task-based language education: From theory to practice* (pp. 129–150). Cambridge: Cambridge Applied Linguistics.

Shaffer, D. W., Squire, K. R., Halverson, R. & Gee, J. P. (2004). *Video games and the future of learning.* Madison: University of Wisconsin-Madison and Academic Advanced Distributed Learning Co-Laboratory.

Shang, H.-F. (2003). *The effects of email dialogue journaling on the enhancement of students' reading achievement.* Paper presented at the Fourth Annual Wenshan International Conference, Taipei, Taiwan.

Shetzer, H. & Warschauer, M. (2000). An electronic literacy approach to network-based language teaching. In M. Warschauer & R. Kern (Eds.), *Network-based language teaching: Concepts and practice* (pp. 171–185). Cambridge: Cambridge University Press.

Silberman, S. (1997). *Physics in the 1960s: PLATOFest.* Retrieved December 8, 2010 from <http://physics.illinois.edu/history/PLATOfest.asp>.

Skiba, D. J. (2007). Nursing education 2.0: Second Life. *Nursing Education Perspectives, 28*(3), 156–157.

Smith, D. B. (2001). *Taking students to task: Task-based computer-mediated communication and negotiated interaction in the ESL classroom* (Unpublished doctoral dissertation). The University of Arizona.

Smith, B. (2003). The Use of Communication Strategies in Computer-Mediated Communication. *System, 31*(1), 29–53.

Snookes, P. (1995). Using the Internet for interactive text-based communication and learning. *CALL Review: The Journal of the IATEFL Computer Special Interest Group*. Retrieved March 2, 2008 from <http://.iatefl.org/calrevnv.html>.

Sproull, L. & Kieller, S. (1991). *Connections: New ways of working in the networked organization*. Cambridge: MIT Press.

Steinkuehler, C. A. (2004). *Learning in massively multiplayer online games*. Paper presented at the International Conference on Learning Sciences, Santa Monica, California.

Stephenson, N. (1992). *Snow Crash*. New York: Bantam Spectra.

Stockwell, G. & Levy, M. (2001). Sustainability of e-mail interactions between native speakers and nonnative speakers. *Computer Assisted Language Learning, 14*(5), 419–442.

Sullivan, N. & Pratt, E. (1996). A comparative study of two ESL writing environments: a computer-assisted classroom and a traditional oral classroom. *System, 29*(4), 491–501.

Sykes, J. M. (2008). *A dynamic approach to social interaction: Synthetic immersive environments & Spanish pragmatics* (Unpublished doctoral dissertation). University of Minnesota.

Sykes, J. M., Oskoz, A. & Thorne, S. L. (2008). Web 2.0, Synthetic immersive environments, and mobile resources for language education. *CALICO Journal, 25*(3), 528–546.

Taylor, T. L. (1999). Life in virtual worlds: Plural existence, multimodalities, and other online research challenges. *American Behavioral Scientist, 43*, 436–449.

Taylor, T. L. (2002). Living digitally: Embodiment in virtual worlds. In R. Schroeder (Ed.), *The social life of avatars: Presence and interaction in shared virtual environments* (pp. 40–62). London: Springer.

Thomas, P. & Carswell, L. (2000). Learning through collaboration in a distributed education environment. *Educational Technology & Society 3*(3), 373–383.

Thorne, S. (2006). Pedagogical and proxiological lessons from internet-mediated intercultural foreign language education research. In J.A. Belz and S.L. Thorne (Eds.), *Internet-mediated intercultural foreign language education* (pp. 2–30). Boston: Thomson Heinle.

Thorne, S. L. (2008). Transcultural communication in open internet environments and massively multiplayer online games In S. Sieloff Magnan (Ed.), *Mediating discourse online* (pp. 305–327). Amsterdam: John Benjamins.

Thorne, S. L., Black, R. W. & Sykes, J. M. (2009). Second language use, socialization, and learning in Internet interest communities and online gaming. *The Modern Language Journal, 93*, 802–823.

Thorne, S. L. & Payne, J. S. (2005). Evolutionary trajectories, internet-mediated expressions, and language education. *CALICO Journal, 22*(3), 371–397.

Thurlow, C., Lengel, L. & Tomic, A. (2004). *Computer mediated communication: social interaction and the internet.* Thousand Oaks, CA: SAGE Publications.

Tudini, V. (2003). Conversational elements of online chatting speaking practice for distance language learners? *Apprentissage des Langues et Systemes d'Information et de Communication (ALSIC), 6*(2), 83–99.

Tudini, V. (2003). Using native speakers in chat. *Language Learning & Technology, 7*(3), 141–159.

Vinge, V. (2001). True Names. In: Frenkel, J. (ed.), *True names and the opening of the cyberspace frontier* (pp. 239–330). New York: TOR.

Vygotsky, L. (1962). *Thought and Language* (E. Hanfmann & G. Vakar, Trans.). Cambridge: The M.I.T. Press.

Vygotsky, L. (1978). *Mind in society: The development of higher mental processes.* Cambridge: Harvard University Press.

Wachowski, A. & Wachowski, L. (Writer) (1999). *The Matrix* [film].

Wang, A.-L. J. (1997). *Bridging the cultural gap through computer-mediated cross-cultural communications: A case study of Chinese college students in Taiwan* (Unpublished doctoral dissertation). New York University

Wang, Y. (2004). Supporting synchronous distance language learning with desktop videoconferencing. *Language Learning & Technology, 8*(3), 90–121.

Wankel, C. & Kingsley, J. (Eds.) (2009). *Higher education in virtual worlds: Teaching and learning in Second Life*. Bingley: Emerald Group Publishing Limited.

Ware, P. D. (2004). Confidence and competition online: ESL student perspectives on web-based discussions in the classroom. *Computer and Composition, 21*(4), 451–468.

Ware, P. D. (2005). "Missed" communication in online communication: Tensions in a German-American telecollaboration. *Language Learning & Technology, 9*(2), 64–89.

Warschauer, M., Turbee, L. & Roberts, B. (1996). Computer learning networks and student empowerment. *System, 24*(1), 1–14.

Weber, A., Rufer-Bach, K. & Platel, R. (2007). *Creating your world: The official guide to advanced content creation for Second Life*. Indianapolis: Wiley.

Weinbaum, S. (1935). *Pygmalion's Spectacles*. Wonder Stories: Project Gutenberg. Retrieved July 15, 2010, from <http://www.gutenberg.org/etext/22893>.

Weininger, M. & Shield, L. (2003). Promoting oral production in a written channel: An investigation of learner language in MOO. *Computer Assisted Language Learning, 16*(4), 329–349.

Williams, L. F. (2003). *The nature and complexities of chat discourse: A qualitative case study of multi-level learners of French in an electronic environment* (Unpublished doctoral dissertation). The Pennsylvania State University.

Winder, D. (2008). *Being virtual: Who you really are online*. Chichester: John Wiley & Sons, LTD.

TELECOLLABORATION IN EDUCATION

Edited by
Melinda Dooly & Robert O'Dowd

The series' focus is on the pedagogical processes and outcomes of engaging learners in different geographical locations in virtual contact and collaboration together. This contact can take place through the application of online communication tools such as e-mail, synchronous chat and threaded discussion as well as the tools of Web 2.0: like wikis, blogs, and online publishing. The series is also particularly interested in innovative teaching practices involving telecollaboration that integrate the use of newly emerging forms of Internet tools such as social networking or 3D virtual worlds.

A major aim is to reflect the diversity of research and practice in this area of knowledge, providing a space for transversal dialogue among teachers and teacher trainers, administrators, researchers, and educators working in different subject areas as well as various areas of education.

Telecollaboration in Education deals with the application of such activity in different subject areas (e.g. Foreign Languages, History, Science) and in different educational contexts, including but not limited to primary, secondary, university and adult education. Publications within the series include scholarly monographs and collected papers editions as well as cutting-edge projects that exemplify good practice in the application of distanced collaborative efforts. Training manuals for educators in the organisation and application of telecollaboration are also a possible type of publication within the series. Language of publication is English.

Vol. 1 Sarah Guth & Francesca Helm (eds)
Telecollaboration 2.0. Language, Literacies and Intercultural Learning in the 21st Century.
2010. ISBN 978-3-03943-0440-5

Vol. 2 Randall Sadler
Virtual Worlds for Language Learning. From Theory to Practice.
2012. ISBN 978-3-0343-0573-0